What peoj
Ordinar

I love this book! I'm a fan of this book! It's so powerfully moving and so well written. You can't leaf through this book. I just kept turning page after page You're in the room with Patrick when things are happening. You're in his brain. You're in his heart. If I were at a seminar, I would say I don't want anyone to leave this room without this book. This book is really worth reading. You're going to love it, and it will impact you in a beautiful way. *Ordinarily Extraordinary* is a book I think should be on everyone's required reading list. Make sure you get this book!

Jack Canfield
Co-Author of the bestselling *Chicken Soup for the Soul* series
A pioneer in the field of Personal Development and Peak
Performance

A page turner of a true story, Patrick P. Long evokes raw emotion in the telling of his wife's ordeal with cancer. To have been through this burdensome journey with her, and yet have the presence of mind to write so detail-oriented, clearly and articulately is a gifted writer. A love story and memoir combined, *Ordinarily Extraordinary* was raw, tender and vulnerable.

Long writes with a paint brush as he evokes emotion and metaphors that are rife with description.

This is Long's first book; however, I sincerely hope it won't be his last.

Carol Fitzgerald
Health Care Advocate and author of 6 books, her most recent:
Living a Vibrant Life at Any Age:
Creating Love, Joy, and Connections in Everyday Moments.

Patrick P. Long answers the call to life's many questions, bringing his family's personal story of tragedy and triumph alive in a way that gives voice to one's innermost fears, insecurities, and doubts. This book takes you on an enlightening journey of loving another through life's bumps in the road, pulling back the curtain to the paradox of the perfection of imperfection. A must read that will truly tug at your heart and soul.

Dr. Cheryl Lentz
Keynote Speaker, Best Selling Author
www.DrCherylLentz.com

In working with cancer patients and their families for decades, I found Long's story as real and compelling as it gets. *Ordinarily Extraordinary* takes you on a journey wading through the complexities and pain so many experience when faced with a cancer diagnosis. Each page captures the true essence of his wife and her keen ability to create extraordinary moments and connections continuously. As the story unfolds, it weaves into an unexpected journey of love, loss, anger, survivorship and personal growth. Long truly sets "The Tone" of how a family moves forward after such a loss. Incredibly inspiring, and I can't wait to read it again!

Stephanie Hadfield
Sr. Manager, Community Development of the
American Cancer Society

Raw. Real. Revealing.

Ordinarily Extraordinary is a compelling account of one man's experience with the realities of love, advocacy, caregiving, and loss. Long's story of his wife's encounters with cancer, strokes, and communication challenges is captivating. We often hear and read these accounts from survivors, which are poignant. But this one exposes the heart and nerve of a dedicated husband struggling to keep it together as he witnesses his wife's steady decline. What struck me most was his enduring devotion to his wife, whom he calls "ordinarily extraordinary." With humor and humility, he lets us see how the ordinary can lead to extraordinary outcomes.

María Tomás-Keegan
Certified Career & Life Coach | Specialty: Transitions
www.TransitionAndThriveWithMaria.com

Do you want to see the extraordinary aspects in your seemingly ordinary life? Look no further! In *Ordinarily Extraordinary,* Patrick P. Long lovingly and candidly shares profound experiences as a husband, father, and best friend. When reading *Ordinarily Extraordinary*, we have the privilege to take a front row seat and learn from a gifted, transformational role model. This is a genuine love story about life, and even more importantly, about hope. With this inspirational book by your side, you will have the opportunity, as well as the motivation, to become the best version of yourself, to become the person you truly want to be.

Wendy K. Benson, MBA, OTR/L and Elizabeth A. Myers, RN
Co-Authors, *The Confident Patient*
2x2 Health: Private Health Concierge
http://www.2x2health.com/

After years working with children who have a parent with cancer and now as a nurse, I've gotten small glances into the day-to-day struggles that come along with a cancer diagnosis. This novel puts you right in the hospital room as Patrick P. gives a raw and emotional account of one of the most difficult situations a family can face.

I couldn't put it down—definitely a must read and a poignant tribute to an incredible wife, mother, and friend. Long's story is captivating and full of depth, at times dark, funny, sad, yet ultimately uplifting and inspirational.

Mary Graeber,
Camp Kesem Alum and RN

ORDINARILY EXTRAORDINARY

LOVE AND ANGER

LIFE AND DEATH

HOPE AND INSPIRATION

Patrick P. Long

Paddy P Publishing

Ordinarily Extraordinary
Love and Anger, Life and Death, Hope and Inspiration
Patrick P. Long
Paddy P Publishing

Published by Paddy P Publishing, LLC, St. Louis, Missouri

Editor: Karen L. Tucker, CommaQueenEditing.com

Creative Editor: Cheryl Roberts Oliver

Project Management and Book Design: Davis Creative, DavisCreative.com

Amazon Best Seller Marketing Campaign: Rebecca Hall Gruyter, YourPurposeDrivenPractice.com

PR/Marketing Consultant: Kristy Barton, sunshinemultimediallc.com

Cover Photo: Ian Everett Didriksen, MountEverett.video

Website Design and Development: Rachel Dolan, BoostItStudio.com

Publisher's Cataloging-In-Publication Data
(Prepared by The Donohue Group, Inc.)

Names: Long, Patrick P., author.

Title: Ordinarily extraordinary : love and anger, life and death, hope and inspiration / Patrick P. Long.

Description: St. Louis, Missouri : Paddy P Publishing, [2020]

Identifiers: ISBN 9781735105505 | ISBN 9781735105512 (ebook)

Subjects: LCSH: Long, Melanie (Melanie Kay), 1974-2019. | Cancer--Patients--Biography. | Cerebrovascular disease--Patients--Biography. | Long, Patrick P.--Family. | Grief. | Loss (Psychology) | BISAC: BIOGRAPHY & AUTOBIOGRAPHY / Personal Memoirs. | FAMILY & RELATIONSHIPS / Death, Grief, Bereavement. | FAMILY & RELATIONSHIPS /General. | LCGFT: Biography.

Classification: LCC RC265.6.L65 L66 2020 (print) | LCC RC265.6.L65 (ebook) | DDC 362.196/9940092--dc23

ATTENTION CORPORATIONS, UNIVERSITIES, COLLEGES AND PROFESSIONAL ORGANIZATIONS: Quantity discounts are available on bulk purchases of this book for educational, gift purposes, or as premiums for increasing magazine subscriptions or renewals. Special books or book excerpts can also be created to fit specific needs. For information, please contact Paddy P Publishing, info@paddyppublishing.com

*Dedicated to The Grest, the kids,
and all of Melanie's Minions*

Table of Contents

1 A Stroke of the Ordinary. 1

2 The Uplifting F-Bomb 24

3 Backstories and Tangents 37

4 Toughness Defined. 64

5 The Chemo Party 90

6 The Cowbell Guy 112

7 Mystery Episodes Explained. 132

8 Rebound and Relapse 147

9 Janis and Bobby 169

10 The Tone of the Extraordinary. 199

11 The Middle Pieces 213

About the Author. 231

1

A Stroke of the Ordinary

If anyone had been watching me, everything would have appeared completely ordinary. A typical middle-aged man pulling into a non-descript grocery store parking lot in a cookie-cutter minivan. My size was the only thing that might have stood out, since I stand 6'5" with a large build. Otherwise, it all would have appeared to be an uneventful trip to the store on a dull midwestern evening in suburbia. Just another boring middle-aged dad living his average, mundane, humdrum life.

Despite one recent development that we'd been informed was well under control, we were right back to our ordinary life. It had been another little bump in the road, and we had grown pretty accustomed to the bumps. In our own version of special relativity, this was the normal routine. This was our ordinary. I walked into the grocery store to pick up some bread and milk, a prescription for my wife, and a couple of things she needed. Somewhere between the apples and bananas, not too far from the rhubarb, my phone rang. Walking through the grocery store, my phone rang. Moments don't get much more ordinary than that.

I pulled my phone out of my pocket and saw that it was my wife, Melanie, calling. I went to the grocery store because she asked me to get a few things while she took a shower. Being the obedient husband, as we liked to joke, I went. When I saw it was Melanie calling, I figured she had thought of something else she wanted or we needed.

"Hey," I answered.

The line was silent for a few seconds.

"Are you there? Can you hear me? I can't hear you if you can hear me." This was also annoyingly ordinary and typical. Our cell phone reception glitched, or completely dropped, far too frequently, especially with how much we paid for service every month. "Stupid technology," I grumbled.

"Cominee," she said.

I instantly spun on my heels back toward the front door. The thing that terrified me was the clarity of that strange word. I could tell it wasn't a connection problem. I could hear the intricacies of her voice too clearly. I could hear the exertion to get that single mangled word out. I desperately wished it was a bad connection. I desperately wanted it to be stupid technology. Instinctively, I knew better.

"What's wrong? Can you speak?" The tremors of fear in my voice must have been rolling like waves through the store. I felt as though I'd been marooned in the produce section, immediately feeling guilty and stupid for leaving her home alone in her condition, but I thought—we thought—her condition was stable. We were told things were under control. But the thing about guilt is, it doesn't care what you thought or how good your intentions were. Guilt comes to the party regardless.

"Um," came a grunted utterance through the phone. I struggled to hear what she was struggling to say. I felt like I was trying to push my head into the phone to get closer to her and hear more clearly. "Eng." As seconds passed, I desperately wanted to say something, find something to say to fix everything and help her. I felt as powerful as a blade of grass in a tornado. I didn't want to interrupt her or miss what she was painstakingly trying to verbalize. I remained resolutely silent and listened intently. "Rung," she finally said.

It didn't matter how staggered and garbled her articulations were. "Um – eng – rung," was clearly "Something's wrong," and it provided the terrifying but mostly unnecessary confirmation that we did not have a bad connection.

"I'm heading back home. I'll be there in a couple minutes." Panic does not roost easily in me, but I was now panicked to capacity and sickened by the realization that my voice was quivering. I didn't want Melanie to hear anything like that. I knew she was terrified, and I didn't want my fear amplifying her fear, but I couldn't control it.

The moment wasn't quite so ordinary any longer, and I'm sure I didn't look mundane and humdrum on the way out. With a tunneled focus, I bolted out of the store, dashed across the parking lot, dove into our minivan, and pulled out of the parking space. I told myself to keep it together. I didn't want to make a horrible situation worse by slamming into another car or something even more unthinkable than that. I rallied against the shock and terror to retain some situational awareness and prevent exponentially escalating the chaos.

The near silence on the other end of the line was horrifying. It was made worse as the only utterances I could hear sounded like her fighting just to breathe, although I couldn't tell what I was actually hearing. Visions of her collapsed in the shower with her head bleeding profusely from hitting the edge of the bathtub filled my head. I realized she wouldn't have the phone with her if that had been the scenario. Was it something worse than that? It was as if my mind was short-circuiting with one horrible thought after another, guilt for thinking such horrible thoughts, disgust with myself for not handling the situation better. Myriad such thoughts and feelings attacked my psyche like a swarm of stinging wasps in mere seconds.

"All…ine…un," Melanie finally said. I sensed that our normal, our ordinary, had already passed through another phase shift. Our lives would never be the same, yet again.

"Okay!" I exclaimed, my quivering voice persistently belying my desire to stay strong and positive for her. Her idea to call 9-1-1 was better than my idea to drive her to the emergency room, which at least told me she was thinking clearly if not communicating clearly. Instead of taking the time to drive to the hospital and go through emergency room procedures and waiting time, emergency responders could immediately assess and treat her, likely calling ahead to the hospital for any incoming needs. Her rational thinking eased my mind slightly—but only slightly.

"I'm hanging up now and calling 9-1-1," I practically shouted into the phone, both out of panic and intentionally to be sure she would hear me and know what was happening. I hung up, held the button for Siri, and said "Call 9-1-1."

I had never used Siri before to call 9-1-1, but before I could even wonder how quickly the call would get through, a young man's voice was on the line asking me what my emergency was. The dispatcher was impressively professional. I explained what was happening. He asked a few quick clarifying questions and reassured me that responders had been dispatched. He instructed me to concentrate on driving and getting back to my wife right away. The drive home was maybe three minutes, and the call was over by the time I was halfway there.

I pulled up along the street curb near our house a minute later. I thought to leave plenty of room for emergency vehicles and not block their access. I sprung out of the car and ran to the door, wondering where and how I would find Melanie. Terrifying scenarios continued to flash through my head—horrible images contorting in my mind. I hated it, but I couldn't prevent the thoughts and feelings.

It was simultaneously a great relief and a great terror to see her sitting on the sofa. She had managed to get herself there, which was a great relief as another good sign that she could still think and function. It was a great terror because she looked terrified, her eyes wide and full of fear. She was perched on the edge, laboring to breathe, and holding her right arm out over her leg in a strange way.

"Et..." She laboriously gulped for air and fought to form her words. "Eye...ant," she said.

I felt horrible for not understanding her. I didn't want to frustrate her, but I had no idea what she was saying this time. I shook my head and held my hands out, palms up, at my sides.

Was this really happening?

She made eye contact with me and then deliberately lowered her head and exaggeratedly looked down at her lap.

"Ants," she said.

"Oh!" She was sitting in a T-shirt, but I now noticed that she was naked from the waist down.

Pants. She had been trying to say, "Get my pants."

I heard the first sirens in the distance, and I knew she didn't want the emergency responders to encounter her like that. The local police and fire stations were only a couple miles away, so they would be to our house quickly.

As I went up the hall, she made a garbled but deliberate sound. It wasn't a formed word, and I couldn't reproduce the sound, but I knew what she was trying to say. After nearly 19 years of marriage, I spoke Melanie in all its forms.

"Yeah," I shouted back, trying not to sound frantic as I rushed to our room, "I'll get underwear."

I pillaged the drawers in her dresser and found pants and underwear, dashed back down the hall, and helped her pull the underwear up on her thighs. The sirens were noticeably louder. They would be here momentarily.

I grabbed the pants and she shook her head. I was confused. Was she losing more cognitive ability? She was still holding her right hand on her leg oddly, but her left hand was okay. With her left hand, she waved at the pants and shook her head again.

I looked at her confused. The sirens wailed louder; from the sound of them, they were likely near the top of our street. With her eyes, she exaggeratedly looked up the hallway and waved at the pants with her left hand again.

"*Really*?" I exclaimed. "*Seriously!*"

I instantly felt like an asshole. This wasn't the time to question her wishes or make her feel bad about anything.

She nodded. She was serious.

I went back up the hall, struggling to pretend I was in control yet infinitely more flustered. I plundered and pillaged and found a different pair of pants, all while the sirens screamed so loudly it seemed they might be parked on our front porch.

I want to take a moment and make sure you clearly understand something. This story is true. It is not *based* on true events. It is not *inspired* by a true story. Those always seem to be the words used at the beginnings of "true" stories, like a disclaimer to prevent lawsuits in our litigation-crazed society, but I'm not hiding behind disclaimers. I changed a few names because I encountered some people whose names I never knew or couldn't remember. Otherwise, this story is completely and entirely 100 percent true.

This whole pants thing—it really happened. In the middle of a horrifying medical emergency with responders nearly on our doorstep, I was sent back up the hall for acceptable pants while she sat with her underwear pulled only halfway up her thighs.

I don't think I could make that up.

I dashed back down the hall. These pants apparently met her approval, so I pulled them over her feet and started them up her legs. She grabbed onto my arm with her left arm, and I helped her up. Together, we pulled the underwear and the acceptable pants up over her hips. It was already dark, and the lights from the emergency vehicles splashed in through the open front door and swirled over our walls. Melanie settled back onto the sofa. I heard the responders approaching the front door, only steps away. I hopped over and pushed open the screen door, and then backpedaled quickly so I wouldn't impede them. I didn't want one second wasted. I wanted them at her side. We needed them at her side. Thank God for them.

They immediately began asking her questions, but she couldn't answer. While I was so deeply grateful and had some sense of relief that they were on the scene and attending to her, she seemed to have totally lost the ability to speak, and the terror flared back up as her speech, and therefore her condition, worsened.

What was happening to her?

■ ■ ■ ■ ■ ■

This event with Melanie occurred about two weeks after my 50th birthday, and I had no direct experience or knowledge of seizure or stroke until a few weeks earlier when my mom suffered a stroke. It was an unexpectedly relevant experience that helped me minimally understand and cope with what was happening to Melanie.

My nieces had gone to my mom's house and found her on the floor of her bedroom, unable to move. She was likely in that state for at least several hours. We called 9-1-1 that night also, which had led to a lengthy hospital stay. I was unfortunately becoming far too accustomed to lengthy hospital stays.

We were advised to have someone stay with our mom as much as possible during the first few days of her hospital stay, so we took shifts, including overnight. I stayed with her on the first night, and she suffered a seizure. It was a sickening experience watching her body contort and listening to her incoherent ramblings. The entire experience was as educational as it was distressing.

I immediately called the nurses. A couple of them were in the room quickly, but it was disconcerting and shocking to see how they reacted. They hardly did anything. They mainly watched her. They discussed their observations while remaining quite calm in their relative inaction. My initial gut reaction was that they were incompetent, inept, and calloused. I wanted to yell at them to do something for her, yet I knew that was an emotional reaction. I had to convince myself to trust that they were doing the best they could. As was increasingly normal, I was in the middle of something that I didn't understand.

After her seizure subsided, they said the staff doctor was starting his rounds on the floor. Within minutes, my mom began having another seizure. One of the nurses immediately went for the doctor, and he arrived quickly enough to observe the last half of her seizure. I was again stunned by his lack of action. The only action he took was cocking his head slightly to the side as he watched her convulse. I was dumbfounded. He appeared like someone seeing something mildly interesting on the television and stopping to watch for a minute. There was no urgency, no directives, no orders to the nurses to do something—to do *anything!*

When the second seizure subsided, he began to discuss actions with the nurses. I think he told them to administer some drug and a few other instructions, but I couldn't comprehend their casual attitude and approach. I wanted to see them theatrically scurrying about like they do on all the medical television shows, intensely barking dramatic commands and making sensational statements with expressions of unrestrained gravity strewn across their faces.

This instance of reality didn't mesh with the on-screen world.

While struggling to be as respectful as I could, I questioned the doctor about what was happening once the waves of the event dissipated. I minimally understood his explanations. When he left, I questioned the nurses, and my understanding progressed but, again, only minimally.

In the days that followed, I did my own research, including speaking to family members and friends with more experience and knowledge in these areas. I questioned doctors and nurses during subsequent hospital visits. I came to understand that strokes and seizures are not like other medical emergencies. If someone is choking, you can use methods, such as the Heimlich maneuver, to dislodge the obstructing object, and you can and should do this immediately. If someone is drowning, you can take immediate action, including breathing into their airways to get them to cough out ingested water. You can restart a heart. You can stop bleeding. But while strokes and seizures are very different medical episodes, they have one key aspect in common, which is the unfortunate fact that there is little or nothing you can, or should, do about them when they are occurring, except in severe instances. Typically, the only things that could be done to abate them are incredibly risky and last-resort options that can lead to a slew of other, and possibly fatal, side effects.

In my mom's case, the prescribed medical treatments helped tremendously. She showed no signs of loss of function and had no more strokes or seizures. In fact, her overall health improved to a higher level than it had been for years, which helped me understand that such terrifying episodes can turn out okay. I learned that the doctors and nurses were doing the only thing they could for her while she was having the seizures, which was to observe and determine the specifics of how the seizure was affecting her so they could properly evaluate how to minimize her chances of these episodes recurring. They hadn't been idly standing by. They were professional observers soaking in an entire battery of information that I had no clue about.

■■■■■■

With my newfound understanding of all this, I had a higher level of trust as to how the responders were dealing with Melanie that night in our living room. But this was different, for a whole lot of reasons. This did not appear to be a seizure. My best guess was a stroke. My primary fear was that it was something worse than a stroke, although I didn't know what that could be. I imagined cancer spreading into her brain and eating away at it, but I made a concerted effort to push those thoughts out of my head.

I remember one of the responders telling Melanie to breathe. They had quickly surmised that due to panic or fighting against what was happening to her, she was reacting in a way that caused her to quit breathing.

"You'll be okay," one of them said to her. "But you need to stay calm and breathe, okay?"

I recall that the confidence, demeanor, and professionalism of the responders were impressive and reassuring—to a degree. There's only so much you can be reassured of in such situations.

"Can you tell me your name?" one of them asked her.

She didn't respond. She looked like she was struggling to find the word, opening her mouth and making a motion as if gulping.

"Keep breathing, okay. I need you to calm down."

Two paramedics stood on either side of her. I was right in front of her, although I'd taken an extra step back to make room. A cop stood at my side, and more firemen lined up between him and the front door. The small living room of our shoebox-sized house was packed. I could hear multiple voices outside the door.

I've noticed emergency calls in the neighborhood before and always wondered why so many of them show up. I thought we only needed an ambulance, but cops and firemen showed up too. Maybe they need to secure the scene until they know what the emergency actually is? This could have been a domestic violence incident or something else, regardless of what the caller told the 9-1-1 dispatcher. All I know is a swarm of responders filled the house and spilled out into the front yard, and I was damn glad they were there.

"Can you tell me your name?" a paramedic asked again.

She again tried but was unable to respond.

"What's her name?" one of them turned and asked me.

"Melanie," I responded.

She appeared to be getting worse. She had lost all ability to speak. Was she slipping away right in front of me? I felt like I might start crying, but I tried to look confident and strong, both for her and because of the group around me.

Here's the stupid part, which I share to be candid: I'm a guy. A typical, ordinary guy in most ways, which is to say that I'm a big stupid male. Being a big stupid male, I didn't want to look weak or cry in front of this group, *especially* this group. Every one of them looked like he should be in one of those beefcake calendars of hot firemen or hot cops they sell for charity. Each guy looked like he spent about five hours a day in the gym. I wasn't focusing on that, but it was hard not to notice. It was more of a sensation than a conscious thought.

Looking like a bunch of buffed-up superheroes, they exuded confidence and professionalism, moving quickly and deliberately. While I wasn't focusing on it or dwelling on it, my feelings of inadequacy emanated from situational awareness. I wanted to be part of this group. I wanted to feel like I belonged—be one of the guys. The little kid in me still wanted to be a fireman, a cop, a brave hero, so I didn't want to reveal my sense of inferiority or inadequacy by crying like some baby in front of them.

See, I told you that was the stupid part. I mean, what an idiot. It's embarrassing to admit, but I'm trying to keep this real and honest. My own absurd stupidity is unfortunately part of this story. Don't we all want to be tough? Don't we all want to be strong and in control? I've learned in life that there are many kinds of toughness. I wanted to be tough, but at 50 years old, I still had toughness-confusion. I didn't know what kind of tough I really wanted to be. At this moment, I wanted to be tough like these guys, but I knew I wasn't.

"Melanie, I really need you to breathe, okay?" one of them said to her. "Just focus on breathing, alright?"

"How long has she been like this?" another one turned to ask me.

"About 15 minutes, but she just got discharged from the hospital a couple hours ago from having a stroke," I informed them.

I didn't wait for them to ask questions. I had information they needed to know, so I started pouring it out for them.

"It was a mild stroke. She actually had the stroke days ago, but it was so mild she didn't realize she had it. She went into the hospital because of leg pain, and when they did tests, they detected that she had had a stroke in the past few days."

They were listening but keeping their eyes on her. I didn't wait for them to ask questions, I just kept informing.

"She was diagnosed with breast cancer three and a half years ago. She's back on chemotherapy now, which started back up a couple weeks ago."

Melanie looked me intently in the eye. I could tell there was something specific she wanted me to tell them. Some piece of information she particularly thought they needed.

"The cancer metastasized. It spread to her bones, and a few months ago, they found a tumor in her liver." I could tell my voice was shaking, which I hated.

Melanie closed her eyes and nodded slightly. I'd hit on the information she wanted them to know. It was the liver diagnosis, which was a crucial piece of information. She was still thinking clearly.

"She did chemo and radiation early on when she was first diagnosed. Later she did chemo pills for a while, and now she's back on full chemo injections."

I paused for only a moment to let that info sink in. I didn't know what was relevant or useful to them right now, but I wanted them to know everything.

"She's had two back surgeries, spinal fusion surgeries. She had a double mastectomy, reconstructive surgery…and, uh…" I felt like I was forgetting something, and I didn't want to leave anything out. Maybe some piece of information would be particularly useful to them. She'd been through so much in the past three and a half years that it was hard to remember it all, especially under stress.

Melanie pointed toward her ribs. I noticed and thought about what it was she was trying to convey to me. I realized she was pointing at her lungs.

"Oh, Wegener's!" I exclaimed. "She was diagnosed and treated for Wegener's the year before her cancer diagnosis. It presented in her lungs."

Wegener's is a rare disease, a type of vasculitis, which is an inflammation of the blood vessels that can affect any organ, causing damage by limiting blood flow to the organ. The cause is unknown. She went through treatment, which was also a form of chemotherapy, so she'd already gone through a round of chemo before she was diagnosed with cancer.

I still felt like I could be forgetting something, but I was pretty sure I'd covered the major stuff.

"What medications is she on?" one of them asked.

As if.

I couldn't have memorized all those if I tried, and I couldn't pronounce half of them. I instinctively turned toward the bedroom, trying to think which drawer or bag "The List" was in. I caught Melanie's eye before I could move. She gestured with her eyes in the other direction. When I looked that way, I immediately knew what she was telling me. When she got home from the hospital, I'd set her bags on the floor near the front door. The List was in there. I wove around the cop and firemen and rummaged through the bags, finding The List in seconds.

I wove back to the paramedic and held out The List for him, lifting page one to make it clear to him that there were two pages. As he took The List and gave it an initial scan, he lifted page one and scanned page two quickly, taking it in. The sheer depth of The List seemed to give him pause. His eyes widened for a moment as he looked back up at me, as if he doubted this list was for real. I was deliberately expressionless. It was what it was. His professionalism gripped him quickly, and he adjusted his expression. I'm sure he had seen many crazy things in his time on this job, but I got the distinct impression he'd never seen a medication list quite like that before. Or maybe he had, and I was imagining things, but The List was insane regardless of his reaction.

The List was currently at 23 medications. At one point, I believe it had been up to 27, but with improvements and changes in her condition, it was down to 23. A few of those were over-the-counter (OTC) drugs, but most of them were prescriptions from her various doctors and specialists, which she had a lot of. Even the OTC drugs were ones that the doctors had recommended or approved. We had multiple bins of drugs in the bedroom grouped into morning, afternoon, and nightly feasts.

She gave me a look, and I knew what she was thinking.

"And she takes marijuana at night to relax and get to sleep," I told them. It was still illegal in Missouri, and we didn't put it on The List, but we wanted them to have all the information.

So, it was really 24.

Such was our norm with cancer and all its side effects. I was at that grocery store a lot as our pharmacy was in there. I probably picked up at least three or four prescriptions, new or refill, per week. The pharmacists were as familiar to me as some of my friends. I knew which shifts they worked and what days they had off. I usually knew which ones I would see depending on which day and what time of day I was making a pickup.

Nobody should be that familiar with the pharmacists unless they work there. I was.

"And she's currently taking all these?" the paramedic asked, his voice even. If there were any hints of his apparent but subtle shock, they were now hidden.

"Yes." I nodded.

Melanie caught my eye again.

"Oh, and blood thinners. They gave them to her at the hospital today. I was on my way to pick up her prescription when all this happened."

So, it was really 25.

"Do you know what blood thinner, or what dose?" He looked at me.

I shook my head and shrugged. The prescription was called in so we didn't have paperwork, and if Melanie knew, she couldn't say right now.

"Keep breathing, Melanie, okay? Focus on your breathing," the other paramedic told her.

"I can watch the kids." I looked up to find our neighbor from across the street, Deb, standing in our doorway.

"They aren't here. They're at her sister's," I told her. Melanie only had one sibling, her sister Stephanie. Stephanie lived about 15 minutes away from us, and the kids had been at her house most of the day.

"How many kids do you have?" one of the paramedics asked. I briefly wondered if this mattered in any medical way, but I answered him.

"Four."

"I can watch the dog for you. You don't need to worry about that," Deb said.

I stared at her blankly. "What dog?"

She pointed toward the floor, and when I looked down, to my surprise, there really was a dog there.

I stared at it for a few seconds, and it started to look a little familiar. After a few more seconds, I recognized and remembered the dog.

When I looked up, the responders were all staring at me with perplexed expressions. I realized that they might think I was losing it, since it appeared that I couldn't even remember my own dog in my own house.

"We're dog sitting," I explained.

We were providers in a dog-sitting service. As Melanie's cancer and treatments and medications took their toll, she had to quit working a regular job, so she looked for creative ways to continue generating income. We registered with an online-managed dog-sitting service a couple years earlier, and we would have a dog or two in our house for a least a couple of days each week. It was nice for the kids as they got to play with dogs they liked, but we didn't have veterinary bills and other hassles. Let the kids play with a dog for a few days, give it back to its owner, and get paid. We made enough to pay for a little vacation each year, which we wouldn't have been able to take otherwise.

After a moment, the responders' perplexed stares faded, and they went back to focusing on Melanie, so I guess they weren't concerned about me losing my shit, as Melanie liked to say.

I scurried into the kitchen, gathered the dog's bowls and food and toys, shoved them in a bag, and gave it all to our neighbor. While I was doing that, I heard a paramedic telling Melanie to breathe again and continuing to talk to her. They were in the process of getting her up and into the stretcher by the time I returned to my post.

"How old are your kids?" the cop standing next to me asked.

"Four, six, eight, and twelve."

He didn't respond. The silence felt awkward. I could have been imagining that, but I doubt it. The hollow reaction had become familiar. What could anyone say to such information? Any response, even the best attempt at a consoling or compassionate statement, was going to sound dreadful, a disconsolate reflection of the looming possibility of the severance of a mother and her four young children. I've discovered this reasonable and well-intentioned question becomes inescapably devastating in its answer.

"Which hospital are we taking her to?" one of the paramedics asked.

"Barnes, on Kingshighway."

They were out the door quickly with the answer. As they maneuvered their way out, I remember the cop putting his hand on my shoulder. I'm not one to either bash cops or blindly support them. I'm pretty darn sure they're human beings like the rest of us. I figure most of them are good people, and some of them are not. I appreciate the good ones and have immense respect for what they do.

This cop seemed to be one of the good ones. When he put his hand on my shoulder, he didn't reach forward in a patronizing manner. He reached up from behind my back, cupping his hand over my shoulder, evoking the camaraderie of devoted teammates leaning on one another in a huddle of solidarity. In that moment, I felt like one of the guys, trusting my cohorts would take good care of my bride of nearly 19 years.

I followed the stretcher down the driveway in the darkness. I was in a haze, but I was coherent enough to decide to drive so I'd have the car. They shut the doors to the back of the ambulance. I stood in the street behind the ambulance looking at her face through the large square windows of the giant metal box on wheels.

She looked terrified. My stomach dropped, and I felt I should be in there with her. *Why was I driving separately? Was it the right decision? I might need the car to get the kids.* I think that was my reason, but I didn't know what was right. No matter what I did, it felt wrong. The whole situation sucked. Cancer sucks.

The paramedic in the back must have asked her something. She looked over at him and nodded slightly. Then she looked out the window into my eyes. Somehow, I smiled. I don't know how I managed to form that smile. I was terrified. Despite the tidal wave of hysterical crying that was about to burst from me, I held it together and smiled.

She blew me a kiss and mouthed the words, "I love you."

She could do that. She could mouth the words. Did she realize she had done that? It was encouraging, even as all this was devastating.

I blew a kiss back and held my hand up in a pseudo-wave. "Love you," I mouthed.

I stood in the middle of the street, feeling heat from the ambulance radiating off the asphalt. The engine growled at me. The multicolored siren lights swirled in flying dots around me. As the ambulance pulled away, I felt like I was stranded on the dance floor at some damned disco of despair.

I had this sinking feeling I would never see her alive again.

I allotted myself about three whole seconds of self-pity and gloom before I cursed myself. I ran inside, chastising myself for thinking negatively and swearing to myself that she would be okay. We'd get through this. She was a fighter. She had battled through so much.

But it felt different this time. Nothing had ever been this urgent or this precarious. When she got the cancer diagnosis, it was shocking and terrifying. Her mom had died of breast cancer when Melanie was nine years old, so it was her worst fear come true. Her diagnosis had, of course, been a stunning blow, but there wasn't a threat of immediate death or loss of faculties, and neither were the myriad other setbacks and obstacles we had encountered in the three and half years that followed.

Treatments had evolved in the decades since her mom had passed. We dealt with it and plowed forward, believing chemo and radiation and other medical treatments and remedies would bring about remission. We were determined to beat this thing, and I always believed she would. We were going to grow old together like we had planned, and hoped, and dreamed.

However, her cancer was aggressive. Even during chemo and radiation, it metastasized, spreading into her bones, and other issues presented themselves after that. All those things I'd rattled off to the paramedics kept happening one by one. What she had endured in the last few years was staggering, but she was still fighting.

Even when we'd found out she'd had a stroke, only days earlier, it had been so minor that she wasn't aware of it when it was happening, which we were told wasn't uncommon. Everything is relative. After three and a half years with cancer, bad news and setbacks became our normal and ordinary. Even her first stroke felt like more of our normal. It was another obstacle, another bump in the road. It had been dealt with. She had a new prescription. The List got one entry longer, and life would keep moving along. Kids still needed to be fed. Laundry still needed to be done. I still had to go to work. There were fears and stresses, but nothing of imminent finality.

Until this point in time, I still believed we'd have at least several more years together, minimum. Although in recent months, that number had dropped. A few months earlier, I believed we would have at least 10 to 20 years. My hope was that during those years, increasingly better treatments, maybe even a cure, would be found, and we'd continue raising our kids and together watch them grow into adults. We'd play with our grandkids together.

I always thought I'd sing that song, "When I'm Sixty-Four," by the Beatles to her when I turned 64. I still had 14 years to practice. I wanted to learn to play the piano. I had a few other songs in mind that I wanted to play and sing for Melanie someday. Another was Paul McCartney's "Maybe I'm Amazed," the lyrics of which became truer with each passing year. Although a goofy daydream, I always thought I'd learn to play the piano and sing those songs to her.

But it felt different this time. It was different this time. Everything had suddenly changed. I felt like her remaining timeline had been instantly erased. Immediacy struck its first blow in that ordinary moment walking into the grocery store, and damn, it was a staggering blow.

I dashed back into the house and grabbed her bags off the floor. The three little tote bags contained clothes and personal items she had wanted during her previous stay in the hospital.

■■■■■

She had been admitted to the hospital due to leg pain the previous Thursday evening. She stayed there over the weekend, celebrating her 45th birthday that Saturday, although it wasn't much of a celebration. We would wait and have a belated celebration when she was better. That was the plan.

Tests had revealed some loss in one of the sectors of her vision. Until they did those tests, she wasn't even aware of the vision loss. The leg pain was due to a blood clot in her leg, and the subsequent tests revealed the stroke. On this day, Sunday, they believed they had it under control. They started her on blood thinners and discharged her. She seemed fine when she got home—at least, relatively fine in that she wasn't any worse or different than she'd been over the past few weeks. We sat and talked for about 30 minutes.

"I meeean..." she started the conversation, "can you believe I had a stroke? Isn't that *weird*? I meeean...what am I, *90*?"

We were laughing and enjoying our time together, discussing and even joking about the absurdity that she had a stroke at 45 years old. I could tell it bothered her a little, but just a little. As she battled through cancer, Melanie would have her share of pity parties, as she liked to call them, but she would bounce back with tremendous spirit. She seemed fine overall. Her spirits were good again—as good as they had been in months.

She'd cracked vertebrae in her back twice in the span of about a year and had undergone two different spinal fusion surgeries about a year apart. She'd spent months sleeping on the recliner sofa because it was both more comfortable and easier to get on and off the sofa than the bed. She was in a wheelchair briefly but had progressed to a cane and then improved to the point where she hardly used the cane. After chemo, radiation, a double mastectomy, chemo pills, spinal fusion surgeries, dozens of drugs and treatments, and more, she adapted and found ways to cope and move forward.

She was a warrior. She never gave up. She never stopped fighting.

The weekend stroke diagnosis was one more bump in the road that hadn't visibly affected her. We wouldn't have even known if they hadn't run the tests. This was the life with cancer that we had adapted ourselves to overcome. This was our ordinary. A new little problem had popped up, and it had been dealt with. We were moving on with our cancer-ordinary lives once again. When I left the house to go to the grocery store, she was getting in the shower. It was just another pleasant cancer Sunday.

The phone call at the grocery store that evening changed everything, and due to the weekend stroke diagnosis, I knew it instantly. We now had an urgent, debilitating, and recurring issue with potentially severe and immediate consequences, something we'd never had before. It felt different this time. It was different this time.

2

The Uplifting F-Bomb

When I came out of the house with her bags, the ambulance's siren was fading in the distance as it sped to the hospital. I got into the car, but I didn't start it immediately. I gripped the steering wheel tightly, dropped my head onto the backs of my hands, and started crying. After a lifetime of wanting to be a tough guy, uncontrollable crying didn't exactly fulfill that aspiration.

It got worse.

I started thinking about how all this was going to affect me. I felt like I was being ambushed by a swarm of ominous and horrific thoughts, like wasps digging their stingers deep into my heart, mind, and soul.

How would I get the kids to and from school each day? How would I have time to shop? Take the kids for haircuts? How would I ever have time to work and still do all these things that she used to do?

The first stroke, which I came to identify as the Vision Stroke, damaged her eyesight. We already knew she would not be allowed to drive for some time, and maybe never again, depending on her ability to recuperate in therapy.

I told myself she wasn't dead, but her condition had deteriorated to a new low. She was currently in the grips of something as least as bad as a more severe stroke, and possibly worse.

She wasn't dead, but I couldn't shake the morbid and terrifying thought that she might be dying, quickly. What if it was worse than a stroke? What if her spreading cancer was finally tearing her down in the final battle of the biological and pharmaceutical war that had been raging in her body for three and a half years, and add another year to that with the Wegener's that preceded the cancer?

How could I ever find another wife? How would I even have time to go on a date while raising four little kids? I desperately didn't want to lose her. I have a habit of naming some of the significant events in my life. One of those was what I called The Escape Clause Revelation, which I'll explain later. The Escape Clause Revelation made me acutely aware of how terrified I was to lose Melanie. It had awoken the fear that I might not get to grow old with my best friend, and now the manifestation of the fear might have arrived.

Along with the fear, I felt the sickening feeling that I was being selfishly hysterical. Why was I thinking the worst-case scenario, and why was I making it about me? Melanie was the one in the ambulance. Was this a normal reaction, or was I the sole, selfish dickhead on the planet? I felt like I was, but I couldn't stop these thoughts and feelings. I feared losing her. I feared for the kids losing their mom. I feared for myself and my life ahead. What would I do if she died? What would I do if she didn't? Was I going to have to take care of four little kids and a disabled woman who used to be my vibrant wife, a 45-year-old who looked and lived like a bald 90-year-old?

"Knock it off," I screamed at myself, pulling and shaking the steering wheel as if I were trying to rip it off the car. "You stupid dick!" I chastised myself. "She's going to be alright."

And with that, my pity party passed. The thoughts pinged in and out of my head in seconds. This entire episode probably didn't last more than a couple minutes, but it was like a couple minutes of holding my hand on a hot stove. I realized that I couldn't control the thoughts and feelings that overcame me, but I could control how I handled them.

Then I said a quick, simple prayer: "Lord, let her be okay, please. I'm asking you for this one thing. Keep her with us, please. I know you can do it."

I have a quiet confidence in God. I don't proselytize. I don't get pious and preachy. I have what I would describe as a scientific viewpoint of God. I believe God created this universe for a reason and put it in motion then lets it take its course. I don't believe He intervenes much at all, which is why so many prayers seem to go unanswered. Melanie prayed many times for her cancer to be taken away, and she had a solid faith, even though she had questions at times. I believe we are meant to make the best out of whatever comes our way and keep trusting in Him that there are bigger reasons we can't comprehend why so much crap keeps happening to us. He isn't cruel to allow bad things to happen, but He knows more than we do and understands why these things must happen in the long run, which is why I always add one last line to any prayer: "But whatever is best, Lord, I accept."

Before I started to drive off, I called Stephanie, Melanie's sister. Not only did I want to tell her immediately what was happening, she also needed to know because she was the one who had our kids. Once the call started ringing through, I pulled from the curb and started to drive.

I took a deep breath as I waited for her to answer, summoning my courage. I knew this would be a hard call to make, but I felt strong and determined.

"Hey," said Stephanie's voice on the line.

With all my strength, courage, and determination—I said absolutely nothing. My throat locked up. I couldn't say the words. I tried to hold my emotions in, but then a guttural blubber noise erupted out of me.

Once again, I felt like the biggest dickhead in the world. I must have been terrifying Stephanie. She handled the whole thing far better than I did. She sounded cool and in control. I finally got out the words that Melanie was maybe having a stroke, all while trying to drive, which I probably shouldn't have been doing. It takes about five minutes to get to the highway from our house. I was almost to the highway by the time I finally explained that something was wrong with Melanie, possibly a stroke, and she was in an ambulance on the way to the hospital.

I also called Tiffani, one of Melanie's closest friends from college. When Melanie had the leg pain a few days ago, Tiffani had taken her into the hospital while I was at work and had spent a lot of the weekend with her. I think the call with Tiffani went about as well as the call with Stephanie, which again made me feel like a pathetic loser and a complete dickhead.

I remember entering the hospital, but I don't remember parking or walking to the entrance. We were lucky and blessed to have Melanie getting her care at Barnes-Jewish Hospital in St. Louis, which is the home of the Siteman Cancer Center, one of the largest cancer centers in the United States and among the best in the world.

As awesome as it is, the hospital is in an area of town that isn't exactly low-crime. Upon entering the emergency room area, I went through security screening, metal detector and all. I emptied my pockets, put my stuff in the little dish, and passed through Melanie's bags. The guard directed me to a counter, and they told me what room and buzzed me through the next door into the hallway beyond the waiting room. I quickly made my way to her room.

Where was she?

She had not been brought to the room yet, and a whole new wave of panic came over me. The ambulance had gotten out way ahead of me and likely sped much faster than I had driven. I had been slowed down even more by parking and security. I had expected them to get her in and back to a room quickly, especially since they had already assigned the room.

So why wasn't she here?

Imagining the worst, I suddenly had trouble breathing. I had the sinking feeling I would never see her alive again when the ambulance pulled away, and now I arrived at her room to find she wasn't there. Her heart had stopped. Another stroke had seized her brain. She wasn't in the room because they were in some surgery room or other room trying to resuscitate her. I could feel it.

"Stop it! Just stop it!" I don't think I actually verbalized those words, but I chastised myself repeatedly with them. Her assigned room was in a back corner of the hallway. It was a unique treatment room unlike an ordinary hospital room. Instead of a door, the entire front of the room was an open entryway with a long white curtain pulled across it. The room was about twice the size of a typical double-occupancy hospital room, with a lot more equipment and cabinets.

I sat in a chair against the far wall and forced myself to take a few deep breaths, which helped. I kept inhaling deeply while staring at a poster on the far wall with the giant title "Thrombosis," a medical term that sounded vaguely familiar, but I didn't know what it was. I couldn't read the poster from that distance, but for some reason, I thought it described a medical procedure for stroke victims. I was curious and considered stepping across the room to read it. But while knowledge can be power, I wasn't sure I really wanted to learn what that poster might teach me.

I realized I should let some other family and friends know what was happening, but I couldn't find my phone. I figured I had left it in my car, so I dug into Melanie's bags and found her phone. That was better anyway, as she would have many more contacts in her phone, including most of my contacts.

I started sending messages to different groups of people, beginning with my family and various friends. I knew Stephanie and Tiffani would spread the word to certain people, so I focused on others who would want to be in the loop. I told people that Melanie possibly had a stroke and provided some basic information. I don't recall what I wrote, but I know I didn't mention my fear that she might have passed. I hadn't lost my shit bad enough to do something that stupid.

After several messages, I saw the curtain flap open and they wheeled her in. She was sitting up with the back of the bed raised high. She still looked scared, but when she looked at me, I silently exhaled volumes of fear. I quickly moved around the bed to an area void of workers or equipment and took her left hand. Her lips were quivering, and her face was set in a look of intense fear. I remember I spoke to her, and she pursed a slight smile at me. I have absolutely no recollection what I said.

Within seconds, staff engaged her. A new one entered the room and went straight to Melanie's other side while the others continued shuffling around and attending to equipment.

"Hey, dear. Can you tell me your name?" I'm pretty sure this healthcare worker was a woman, but I have no recollection of what she looked like. I don't know if she was a doctor, a nurse, or a specialist. With some of them, it's obvious. With others, they wear plain scrubs and you can't tell.

Melanie strained to form the word then shook her head. She couldn't say her own name.

"Do you know where you are?"

She again strained but soon gave up and nodded her head. She probably knew where she was but couldn't form the word or words she wanted to say.

"Do you know what year it is?"

Same reaction.

She appeared to have lost all ability to speak, and I squeezed her hand.

The staff member asked who I was and asked me a bunch of questions about her. We discussed her medical history, current series of events, recent stroke and hospital stay, and more. She also worked Melanie through a series of actions, such as smiling, raising her eyebrows, sticking her tongue out, raising her arms, and more such exercises. I had learned enough about stroke to understand the patient's ability to perform these exercises could reveal information about the type and severity of a stroke, and Melanie performed nearly every exercise perfectly, which felt hopeful.

Many other medical professionals came and went. There were a lot of them. Each one asking her the same or similar questions, with me giving all the answers. She was asked to perform the tongue and eyebrow exercises repeatedly. A parade of variously colored scrubs and lab coats filtered through the room. Even with all the surgeries, treatments, and procedures she'd endured, and with other experiences throughout my life with hospital visits, I had never seen so many different medical professionals rotate through to evaluate one patient, especially in such rapid succession. They just kept coming.

We finally got a break. A group of three of them finished their round of questions and their own variations of the tongue and eyebrow exercises, spoke briefly to one another, and then left the room.

I looked at Melanie and she gazed back intently into my eyes.

She dropped an F-bomb.

It was enunciated perfectly, and it brought smiles to our faces. She seemed to have surprised herself, but it was amazing how soothing and uplifting that F-bomb was. It was one of the best things I had ever heard. Although otherwise incapable of speaking, she still had the ability to drop an F-bomb.

Makes a husband proud.

The smile faded quickly. She looked intently into my eyes again.

"Scared," she said, slightly less articulated but still clear.

"I know," I said. "Me too."

"You…" She got that word out fairly well but then struggled with the next. "Rrrr?"

She playfully feigned surprise, a common game with her, but I could tell there was some legitimacy to it.

"Of course," I said. I tried to sound matter-of-fact, but I couldn't hide the hint of fear.

Once again, I felt like a dickhead, but not entirely this time. From the day Melanie got diagnosed with cancer, I always tried to stay positive and optimistic and show strength and confidence as best I could. To a large degree, that is how I actually felt. It wasn't an act. I believe that every decision, even the best decision, has downsides.

While trying to project strength and optimism, I wouldn't show the fear and concern she needed to confirm that I loved her. From her perspective, if I really loved her deeply, I would be so afraid to lose her that I would be a wreck. While I was aware of this and did let my concern show at times, I still fought to remain as positive and composed as possible. I always felt that was the best mistake I could choose to make.

In this moment, looking into her eyes, I felt the downsides of my decision wringing out my heart. I told her I was scared too, and my eyes teared up. She pursed her lips into a tight smile and started to tear up also. Seeing the fear showed the love, and she needed to see that at that moment.

I squeezed her hand and lowered my forehead against hers. For a few minutes, we leaned gently into one another in relative silence, except for the beeping and buzzing and dinging and hissing and humming of the medical equipment all around us. It was a tender moment that ended too soon when another doctor and another nurse burst through the curtain and began talking to us. I suppose hospital emergency rooms aren't exactly the best places for tender moments.

Dr. Stewart, a neurologist, introduced himself. He asked a battery of questions, mostly the same questions that had now been asked of us multiple times. When Melanie was unable to answer, he directed his questions to me. We discussed medical history, the current series of events, the recent stroke, and whatever else he asked about. He worked her through more tongue and eyebrow exercises. During this session, Melanie interjected and spoke a couple new words, and then surprisingly, a couple more.

"Any other questions for me?" Dr. Stewart asked, signaling that he was done and about to leave.

"Yeah," I said. "What the hell is happening to her?" With all the doctors and nurses and technicians that had been in and out, no one had yet told us specifically what they thought this was. "Is this a stroke, or something else, or what?"

"Yes, it's a stroke," he confirmed.

Finally.

While I didn't want Melanie suffering a stroke, I was somewhat relieved to hear this. I was afraid of something worse like the cancer having spread to her brain. While a stroke was bad, it felt a little less bad than the other possibilities ricocheting around my head.

I asked more questions, including what they would do to treat it or stop it. He mentioned that there were procedures they could do if the stroke were more severe, but those procedures were risky, and her stroke did not seem severe enough. I thought of the thrombosis poster on the wall, but I didn't say anything about that. Later, I was glad I didn't, as I would have been showing my stupidity. I would learn that thrombosis is not a medical procedure but is the term for the formation of a blood clot. I've learned that sometimes it's better to keep my mouth shut and let people believe I might be an idiot than to open it and remove all doubt, as I believe Mark Twain once said or wrote.

While we were talking, I noticed that my brother Martin and his wife Kelly were outside the curtain. I was shocked because I couldn't figure out how they knew where we were or how they could have gotten here so quickly. During the ongoing discussion with the doctor, Melanie continued to regain more of her vocabulary. At one point, she was trying to ask the doctor something. Dr. Stewart was an African American who appeared to be in his early thirties. He was handsome and in good shape, along with being extremely professional and exceptionally intelligent. He looked like he could play a doctor on a medical TV show.

While it was a struggle and took some time, Melanie continued asking him questions. Her speech was rapidly improving. I could tell there was something particular she wanted to know or she wanted to tell him. She had a clear agenda, but it wasn't clear to us. I don't remember how we worked through it, but we finally determined that she wanted to know if this doctor knew another neurologist on staff who had treated Melanie before, someone named Dr. Gahlot. I would have expected two neurologists working in the same hospital to know one another, or at least have heard of one another, but he had no idea who that was. I figured maybe Melanie wanted him to consult with this other doctor on something to do with her stroke, but I also had a gut instinct there was something else going on. The issue was dropped, and Melanie's agenda remained a mystery.

When the doctor left, I told Melanie that Martin and Kelly were here. The nurse stepped up to do something to Melanie, take blood or hook her up to some new gadget or something requiring more privacy, so I stepped out to talk to Martin and Kelly while the nurse performed her task.

I explained the current situation to them, especially making it clear how much trouble Melanie was having speaking. Melanie had conveyed to me that it was embarrassing and she didn't want people to see her like this, but she was okay with Martin and Kelly coming in, so I explained that to them also.

"How did you even know we were here?" I asked Martin while we waited for the nurse to finish her task.

"Well," Martin looked a little perplexed, "you texted us and told us."

"I did?"

I would later recall that I had been texting people while waiting for them to bring Melanie into her assigned room, but at that time, I had no recollection of doing it. I was like a politician accused of some indiscretion like taking bribes or having intercourse with an intern, having no recollection of the event—except in my case, my inability to recall the event in question was actually real.

"But how did you get here so fast?" I asked Martin, and he again looked puzzled.

"That was over two hours ago," he said.

I couldn't comprehend it. I would have sworn we'd only been in that room for about 15 minutes.

"You can come back in now," the nurse called to us.

We immediately went to Melanie's bedside. She was clearly anxious even though she was okay with them being there. She adored them. Martin and Kelly said hi, but it all felt a little awkward.

"Hey, show them what you can do." I glanced at Martin and Kelly as I finished saying this, and they smiled inquisitively.

Melanie didn't hesitate. She knew exactly what I meant.

Looking right at them, she dropped that uplifting F-bomb again, loudly and perfectly enunciated.

Everyone laughed, and the awkwardness melted away.

"She lost all ability to speak for a bit," I told them, "except she never lost the ability to drop an F-bomb!"

It's odd, but for some reason, I was proud of her for that. It was another indicator that she still had control over her own mind despite the speech difficulties; her mind seemed fully intact, complete with F-bombs and agendas, as usual.

"Where…" Melanie got that word out clearly enough but then struggled with the next word. I instantly knew what she wanted to ask.

"You want to know where their kids are?" I asked her.

She nodded.

Martin commented about this to me later. He was amazed that Melanie was going through this horrible episode and was the one in the hospital, yet she made it about them. She next asked who was watching their kids, and then the discussion continued with question after question about what was going on in their lives. Although she had trouble forming words, she kept interrogating them the way only Melanie could.

It was all about them.

.

3

Backstories and Tangents

When Melanie made it all about Martin and Kelly in the emergency room, it didn't surprise me at all. Melanie prioritized relationships above all else. She lived for others. She cherished people, but she wasn't a pushover. She wouldn't tolerate rudeness.

She proved to be far and away the most genuinely caring person I have ever known. This isn't only true with her closest relationships. She had a rare ability to connect with people quickly and deeply, and she did it by constantly putting others ahead of herself. I have never encountered anyone in my life who could make friends so easily and dive deep into a stranger's world in minutes. It was extraordinary to watch, and I witnessed it far too many times to count. Personal connections were the priority of her life. She wasn't materialistic or vane in the slightest.

In the first year we were together, I got seriously reprimanded for buying her roses on Valentine's Day. She thought that was a waste of money and a shallow symbol. She didn't want store-bought cards for holidays or her birthday. She'd rather have something more meaningful, like a note written from the heart. She didn't want objects *representative* of affection; she wanted to feel the *connection* of genuine affection.

She wanted a fountain Diet Coke.

Seriously. It had to be a fountain drink.

On Valentine's Day or her birthday, she'd rather I brought her a fountain than flowers. On my way home from work most days, I would stop and get her a fountain Diet Coke. This little treat was what she would call an I-love-you present. The fact that I would think of that and make the effort to remember and get her one showed her I loved her and was thinking of her. It could be other things, like a snack she likes or me picking up dinner so she didn't have to worry about it that day. But such little thoughtful acts, not objects, showed I was thinking of her and understood her and what she cherished.

To provide you with the context and perspective to understand her and our relationship, I have to tell you some things about me. After all, while this is a story to honor Melanie, it's actually my story, and how can you understand my story if you don't know anything about me. So, I need to give you some backstory to our backstory, and the backstory of that backstory is about me.

I grew up a kid with practically no self-esteem. I thought everyone else around me was confident and smart and capable, and I felt inferior to everyone. I felt pathetic and stupid and inept most of the time. In the eternal debate of nature versus nurture, I don't know how much nature affected me, but there were certainly plenty of environmental variables that didn't help me. From family to school, I would describe the world I lived in as hypercritical and ultrajudgmental, with loads of anger and unhealthy competitive skirmishes flaring up frequently.

It wasn't all bad, and I've come to grips with the bad parts of my past and overcome my own demons. There were also plenty of great moments and fun times in my childhood. Like everything else in life, it's complicated and seemingly contradictory, which makes it hard to explain or reconcile. I don't like writing this next part, but this is a catharsis.

It has taken me five days to write the next several paragraphs because I fear how this will affect my relationships. I worry that at least one of my siblings might be enraged by the things I'm about to share. I also fear that this will make me look pitiful, like some ungrateful brat who pathetically can't get over his own childhood, but I have to tell you about my mom.

My mom was an extremely high-strung woman who was exceedingly vain and obsessed with what others thought of her and our family. I think she wanted to believe that we were some elite, perfect family that should be the envy of the community. She seemed to have a deranged sense of entitlement—as if we were some sort of royalty—and anything that she saw as harmful to that delusion was intolerable to her. She probably meant well and wanted the best for us. I guess you could argue that this showed she cared about us, but she sure didn't handle it well.

When I would get in trouble at school or anywhere else, or do anything that she perceived as detrimental to the royal family image she had fabricated in her head, she became irate and unhinged. She would scream hysterically at me and tell me things like I was an embarrassment and that I should be disgusted with myself. She would tell me I was a burden to her. She would tell me I was fat and a disgrace. She would tell me I should try to be like some friend of mine or some other person, and on and on. I vividly recall her saying these things and many more such things to me many times over the years.

Later in life, I read parenting and child psychology books that explained things a parent should and should not say to a child, and she pretty much covered the full spectrum of saying to me all the things that a parent should never say to a child. Most of the things she said to me I would never, ever say to my own children—not in a million years.

I know others have suffered far worse. In some ways, this wasn't even that bad. But it sure didn't do me any good. It devastated me. Over the years, I talked to Melanie about this at least a few times. Early in our relationship, when we were getting to know each other and talking about our pasts, I would share things about my mom. Melanie doubted if it was all that bad. She questioned if the things I told her about my mom were true, or at least if they were accurate or telling the full story. It's funny how people will doubt you, but I get that. I've certainly doubted the stories of others at times. After she got to know my mom better, she came around to believing every word of what I had told her.

Before she got to know my mother, Melanie once challenged me to admit it wasn't that bad by asking me to share a good memory of my mom. I guess she was trying to force me to admit that it was better than I was claiming. She wanted me to recall something specific about my mom and me that was special and I remembered fondly. I couldn't recall a single thing, and I really tried.

After I tried and tried, I recalled times sitting around the dinner table laughing or in the car laughing and seeing my mom laugh, but these times had almost nothing to do with me and her. This was the family group having some good moments. I finally recalled one thing. My mom exclusively wore full-length skirts. She once bought a pair of jeans, but she only wore them a couple times and then I never saw those jeans again. One day, a couple of my siblings and I were out somewhere with her, and we somehow started racing one another. We were sprinting across some parking lot or field, and I raced my mom, in her jeans, a couple times.

I remember being happy and having fun that day, and now you know the full collection of the wonderful memories I have with my mom throughout my childhood. Pretty touching, isn't it? It warms the heart.

Maybe the biggest defining characteristics Melanie possessed were her ability to make friends and to see the good in people. I have never known anyone else who could draw out the absolute best in people and appreciate and enjoy time with them the way Melanie could. Over the years, I came to defer to Melanie's judgment. If Melanie spent any amount of time with someone and didn't like them, which didn't happen very often, I knew I didn't need to bother with that person. I came to believe that if someone couldn't get along with Melanie, there was something seriously wrong with that person. I would never meet someone Melanie didn't like and find that she just misunderstood them. Her judgment of people was impeccable. Melanie came to find my mom to be an extremely odd and overly unpleasant woman. She did not enjoy time with her, and that is all I need to know to feel validated in my feelings toward my mom.

Of course, my upbringing wasn't just about my mom. I was raised Catholic and attended Catholic schools in which we were taught that everything was a sin and we should live in constant guilt and shame. I recently had lunch with a couple of good friends, and one of them recounted a story that sums this up pretty well. When we were in third grade, we were going into church. Our teacher was a nun—a *nasty* old one. My friend told her he was feeling sick, but she refused to accept that and made him go to church with the class. We went to communion, which was required, and he took the host. If you aren't

Catholic or religious and don't know what that means, it's the bread that represents Jesus. As soon as my friend ate the host, he could feel he was about to throw up. He hurried out of church into the boys' bathroom. The nun followed him out and into the bathroom, and he began throwing up in a urinal. As he was throwing up, she screamed at him that he was throwing up Jesus Christ while slapping him around and admonishing him for sinfully puking out Jesus.

I meeean…how do you do that to a little boy? He wouldn't have ever taken communion in the first place if she had listened to him when he told her he was feeling sick, but this was our world. And that is just one story of many. When something like that happened to me or one of my siblings and my mom would hear about it, she would never take our side. We'd simply get in trouble for it again at home, so we were getting it on both ends. It's a wonder any of us came out of that environment able to function as adults in the world.

And that is where this backstory is going. I almost didn't come out of that world able to function as an adult. In high school, I was terrified of everything and everyone. I believed I was a worthless loser incapable of doing anything. I loved sports, but I failed at every sport I tried because I had zero confidence. I was tall, strong, and naturally athletic, but I felt as if every other kid out there was bigger, faster, stronger, smarter, and more capable than me. I thought every coach hated me and only kept me on a team because it was required or something. In reality, the coaches probably were happy to get a big kid like me on the team but were then disappointed by my lack of effort or commitment, which was only because I felt completely out of place and unwanted despite a love of sports and an underlying desire to succeed. I barely kept my grades up enough to avoid flunking out of school.

When I got out of high school, I went to college, but it was more of the same, except worse. I went to the University of Missouri, Columbia, commonly called Mizzou. Mizzou was known to be a big party school, and I did plenty of that. What I didn't do was attend class or study. I avoided flunking out by withdrawing from my classes on the last day you could withdraw without a grade. The second semester, I did the same. I had some financial aid and worked side jobs and covered my tuition, but it was a big waste of money. I remained in Columbia for a couple more years but mostly kept doing the same thing. In my second year, I actually finished a semester and passed with some credit hours, but then I repeated my pattern in my third year. I kept spiraling out of control and engaging in heavily irresponsible and self-destructive behavior, even though I thought I was having fun most of the time.

I ended up living in some trashed-out apartment with almost no furniture. Fat, drunk, and stupid was my life. I was falling to rock bottom at terminal velocity. I had no purpose in life and didn't believe I was good enough or smart enough to have any purpose. I did have some friends, but they weren't aware of my demons. I faked it, acting like I was having fun and belonging, but I didn't think much of myself. My life was pathetic, a sham, and I was becoming increasingly disgusted with myself every day.

I had some friends over one night for an impromptu party. It went late, and we imbibed heavily, as usual. I don't remember the end of the night, but I woke up the next morning naked on my mattress, which was on the floor without a frame because I didn't have the money for a bedframe. Next to me on the bed was a friend of mine. She was also naked. We had never dated or been romantic or intimate in any way for a bunch of reasons, but it wasn't difficult to guess what had happened.

I climbed off the mattress, threw on some clothes, and went to the bathroom. Seriously hung over, I threw up and then went into the kitchen. Besides all the empty beer bottles, empty beer cans, and trash, the only things I had were two full beers in the fridge and a few stale Cheetos spilling out from an open bag on the counter.

My friend got up. I probably woke her up with all the noise I had made throwing up. She dressed quickly and darted toward the door. We spoke briefly before she headed out, and that was the last I saw of her. I would speak to her on the phone several months later after a mutual friend of ours shared some news with me that would profoundly impact me and my outlook on a great many things for the rest of my life.

After she left, I stood in the kitchen with my head throbbing and contemplated how those two beers and those few stale Cheetos were the sum of all my life savings, possessions, and accomplishments, not discounting the mattress on the floor in the bedroom. Three years of supposedly being a college student and I had passed one semester worth of classes, wasting thousands of dollars. I was no longer falling to rock bottom. I was laying on the rocks.

I went back into the bathroom, leaned on the vanity, and peered into the mirror over the sink. I quickly looked away, unable to look into my own eyes. I felt so pathetic and hated myself. I thoroughly disgusted myself. I was an embarrassment and a disgrace.

Those thoughts hit me, but then I felt something change. A strange surge came up from within me. I looked back into the mirror. I thought about all these feelings I had for myself and why and where they came from, and then I considered why I thought I wasn't as good as anybody else. I wondered why anyone should be considered better than anyone else? We're all just people. We're all human beings. Why couldn't I apply these truths to myself? It suddenly was completely and totally logical to do so. I could succeed at whatever I wanted, and no one could tell me otherwise. I wasn't going to live like this any longer. I would overcome. And then, staring intently into my own eyes, I uttered the words out loud for the first time: *"Don't let the bitch win!"*

Those words felt so real, so right, so true. It was an intense revelation, and the single most important and pivotal moment of my life. Reflecting on it now, I almost hate telling anyone this. It feels sad that I felt that way, but it also rings true. It worked for me. Overall, my life has continued to improve since that day. That was the day I realized that when I hit rock bottom, the thing to do was to use the rocks. I began stacking them to build a tower to climb out of the pit I'd fallen into.

I don't think my use of "bitch" symbolized one woman. I think it also included bullies and others and even my own nature. I wasn't overly bullied in my youth, but kids say cruel things, and I got my fair share of that. But already having an exaggerated sense of inferiority, those same taunts likely haunted me more than some others. It all piled on.

That phrase became my personal rallying cry, but I didn't change in a day. It was a long process that took continued belief, commitment, and persistence. I found the key has been accomplishment. Every accomplishment, big or small, added to my confidence and improved my outlook. Each accomplishment was like a rock that I stacked on the tower.

That day, after staring myself down in the mirror, I contacted Parks College and started the application process. I was surprised I was accepted and so fast. If memory serves, I had my acceptance letter within a couple months. I chose Parks College for a few reasons. It was small and not a party school, so I felt I could focus on studying and be less tempted by partying and the like. I was familiar with Parks as my dad and two oldest brothers went there. Also, the school intimidated me.

It may sound odd that a kid with such an inferiority complex would choose a school that intimidated him, but that was the point. During one of the few stretches when I participated in high school sports, I remember our football coach talking to our team about our schedule. We had one of the toughest schedules in the state. Most teams schedule at least a few weak teams on their schedules to get some easy wins, but our schedule was made up almost exclusively of the top teams in the area. Our coach explained that he wanted us to be challenged because he believed that you can only be the best if you beat the best. That was something else that I have always remembered and took to heart. I agree with him, but I had never believed I was capable of being the best, or even capable of being decent at something.

That was why I chose Parks College. If I was going to prove to myself that I could respect myself, I didn't want to take an easy path. Parks College focused on aeronautical and aerospace studies. It was one of the top engineering schools in the country where bona fide rocket scientists were schooled, like Gene Kranz, who was portrayed by Ed Harris in the movie *Apollo 13*. Kranz was the chief flight director for NASA for years and directed numerous missions, including the first landing on the moon on the Apollo 11 mission. Many aeronautical engineers—although it's more fun to call them rocket scientists—who built our space program were Parks College graduates, including my dad. He was one of the rocket scientists who designed and built the Mercury and Gemini space capsules during the race to the moon. The school had been churning out rocket scientists for decades. It doesn't get a whole lot more challenging than that.

As much as I wanted to be challenged, I was also intimidated and terrified. My first semester, I struggled just to learn how to learn again. I hadn't been studying or applying myself in school for a couple years. I passed my classes, but my grades were average my first semester. Then, to challenge myself more, I walked on for the basketball team. It started off like a joke. After a couple years of diving to rock bottom, living on Cheetos and beer, I was a huge, fat blob, as one of my good friends would kindly describe me later. When I showed up for the first day of tryouts, guys actually laughed at me.

The first thing they had us do was run around a field that was almost exactly one mile around. I was pathetically out of shape. I tried to jog but got so winded I had to stop only about one-tenth of a mile into the run. By the time I got to two-tenths of the mile, other guys were already finished. I was so dizzy that I took a knee on the ground.

My chest hurt so bad that I wondered if I was having a heart attack. Then I heard a voice from above. I looked up, my face turned toward the sun, the bright light practically blinding me. I thought maybe I was dead. I had had a heart attack and God was coming to take me, His voice calling out through the light.

Except it turned out not to be God but a guy named Rick, although Rick was an exceedingly confident young man whom we often joked liked to think he's God.

"You okay, man?" he asked. I don't think I answered him because I could barely breathe, but he helped me up and stayed with me around the rest of the lap and back to the gym.

Rick became one of the best friends I've ever had. Rick was my age, and we were both starting college at the age of 22. I was starting college that old because I spent years diving to rock bottom like a pathetic loser. Rick was starting college that old because he joined the Marines and served his country, including serving in Operation Desert Storm. He was everything you would expect in a Marine who had served his country. He was, and is, a stand-up guy who is boundlessly loyal. He was exactly the kind of guy who wouldn't leave a man behind, which is why he was out there walking me in. Years later, Rick would be the best man in my wedding, and I would be the best man in his. As I said earlier, Melanie's judgment on people was something I came to trust absolutely, and Melanie adored Rick.

I stayed around for the tryout practice, but I couldn't really participate. When I showed up the next day, the guys were stunned. No one had expected me back. The assistant coach chuckled and said, "Didn't expect to see you again." I meeean...even the coach was laughing at me.

Luckily for me, Parks College was a little NCAA Division III school, which means it is small and doesn't provide scholarships or even recruit much. The big schools that play on television are Division I, then there's Division II, and then Division III, and Parks was not even good Division III. Parks was lucky to have enough guys try out to have a full roster, so I could stay on the team as long as I wanted. I stayed on. I was on a mission.

During the first month, I mostly watched practice to learn plays and drills. I would go into the weight room and work out after practice, spending as long as I could on the exercise bike and eventually on the Stairmaster. I lost 30 pounds in the first month and started participating in parts of practice. By the end of the second month, nearing the end of the first semester, I had lost over 50 pounds, and to the shock of the coaches and other players, I was fully participating in practices. By the end of the season, I had lost nearly 80 pounds, going from just over 300 pounds down to 224. I was a changed man, and no one was laughing any longer. In the second season, I would go down to 212 pounds, an accomplishment I once thought I could never reach. I was building a base of confidence and self-esteem that I had never had in my life. I kept stacking rocks on the tower.

Of course, I'd be remiss if I claimed only accomplishment and not failure. I learned that the single greatest requirement of accomplishment is failure, and I only began to accomplish things in life when I quit letting the fear of failure deter me. I came to believe that if I wasn't failing, I wasn't trying. While I had previously felt safe not trying to achieve things because I didn't feel a fear of impending failure, I learned that not attempting things was the greatest failure of all. I learned to embrace failure and use it for growth and greater achievement. My failures have been a source of tremendous knowledge and experience, and I'm proud to say I've failed myriad times. I became more afraid to not fail than I was afraid to fail, and my ambitions escalated.

Academically, I continued to improve. Each semester, my grades would get better. I had a group of friends both from the basketball team and from around campus. I started getting a reputation as one of the smart guys. Teammates and others were coming to me for help with coursework. I never imagined that would happen, but it was a heck of a good feeling.

In my third year, I decided to register for an overload of credit hours, but I had to get advisor approval because the schedule I requested exceeded the maximum allowed full-time credit hours. Not only was I requesting an overload, but I had picked all the hardest courses I needed to take. I signed up for Physics, Calculus, Advanced Economics, and I don't remember what else, but I didn't have a single easy elective or blow-off course.

"You're nuts," my advisor said when she looked at my registration card.

"Yeah," I laughed.

"Seriously," she said, "this is too much. Aren't you on the basketball team? You'll never be able to keep up with all this work. How will you have time?"

"That's the point," I told her. "I want the challenge. I have to know I can do it. I gotta prove it to myself."

We continued discussing it. She cautioned against it, but I persisted.

"You're sure you want to do this?" she finally asked.

"One hundred percent," I said, and she signed off her approval, all the while shaking her head.

That semester, for the first time in my entire academic career, I got a perfect 4.0 GPA. Straight A's with the hardest course load I would ever attempt. I graduated cum laude and later went on to earn a master's degree, again graduating with honors. Not bad for the Cheeto-eating pathetic loser of three years earlier who only avoided flunking out of school by withdrawing just in time.

It wasn't easy, and I struggled a lot, especially the first couple years at Parks. Doubt would creep in and those demons would try to resurface and drag me back down. I would be pushing myself through a workout or struggling in my studies and my personal rallying cry would fire me up to fight again. I hate to say it. I feel like it sounds horrible, but every time I felt I couldn't do something, I'd cry out in my head, "Don't let the bitch win," and that would light a fire in me and I would push through, determined to crush my demons and believe in myself, stacking even more rocks on the tower.

I don't hate my mom. That is an important point for several reasons. I think I did hate her when I was younger. I certainly hated the way she treated me. She said cruel things to me and didn't ever seem to want me around. However, I dealt with all that and I overcame it, and I even came to realize that whatever her shortcomings, she did sacrifice and expend a lot of time and effort in raising seven kids. I had six siblings, and we were not a quiet and tranquil bunch.

I don't have much of a relationship with my mom to this day, and I never will. As I write this, she has advanced dementia, and having any semblance of a normal conversation is less manageable than ever. I don't want to see her suffer. During those nights with her in the hospital, I didn't get any satisfaction from seeing her suffer. Watching her have those seizures was miserable and horrifying, and my heart went out for her.

I actually feel sorry for her. Whatever preoccupations she had, which may have been coupled with good, yet misguided, intentions, she suffered from them more than anyone else, even if she didn't realize what she was missing. She tainted and spoiled relationships that could have been wonderful for her, and she lost out more than anyone. She had a wonderful world of exceptionally terrific people around her, and she rarely enjoyed her time with any of them.

That which doesn't kill us may make us stronger, but I've found I must open my mind and my heart to the lessons my hardships taught and then apply those lessons in my life in order to get stronger. Sometimes I gained a simple insight. Sometimes I had to completely shed off the person I was to become the person I needed to be.

Forgiveness is important for many reasons. Forgiveness has done more for me than for those I forgave. When I let go of hate and negativity, it gave me peace. I became a happier person and a better person. It can be difficult to do and takes time, but focusing on the positives and releasing the bitterness have made my life much better.

Now that I'm done with the backstories to the backstory and accompanying tangents, I will get back to the original backstory. You're welcome.

■■■■■■

I was fortunate to meet Melanie at a point in my life when I'd grown into a young man stable and positive enough to handle a healthy relationship. It was about a year and a half after I graduated from Parks College. I still had a lot of growing to do, but I had climbed the tower out of the pit and established a solid foundation for my life. When I met her, it was instantly fun, and the fun continued. We could do anything together and have a blast doing it. I was normally not a big talker, but we could talk for hours on end, and it was boundlessly exhilarating and interesting. But as great as it was, I didn't know where our relationship was going.

We played hooky from work one day to spend the day together. We went to lunch at O'B Clark's, and once again, my life would be drastically altered during a seemingly ordinary event. O'B Clark's is a rather ordinary bar and grill in the middle of St. Louis County and for years has been an extremely popular hangout.

On this day, the place was nearly empty. The only other patrons were a few old men sitting at the bar. I figured they were probably regulars who came there nearly every day and spent their afternoons telling one another the same old stories. We found a table against the back wall and sat and talked nonstop. Our server came and we ordered pizza, a typical and ordinary pepperoni and sausage pizza. O'B's has always had good pizza.

The server put in our order and returned with drinks, and Melanie started joking and talking with him. This started like an ordinary and friendly brief conversation. We learned our server was a college kid who went to one of the local colleges. He appeared to be about ten years younger than me. Melanie was five years younger than me and had only been out of college for about a year, so it made sense that she could still easily relate to a young college kid.

They kept talking until he finally went back to see if our pizza was ready. When he walked away, she didn't miss a beat, asking me questions as if there had never been a break in our conversation. Within moments, were joking and laughing and having fun together. Her smile was radiant.

The server returned with our pizza, and Melanie started joking with him again and firing questions at him in rapid succession. The conversation was friendly and fun but also grew in breadth and depth. Melanie was so engaged with him that she was barely eating. After about fifteen more minutes of nonstop conversation between them, I started feeling a new sensation. While jealousy might be the obvious sensation, that wasn't it. I could have easily interpreted her interactions as flirting, and most guys would have probably been upset and annoyed that she wasn't paying more attention to them.

That wasn't how I was seeing and hearing their conversation, and so it wasn't jealousy. I was overcome by a sense of awe.

I had never experienced anything like this before. Until that point in time, I didn't think people were capable of anything even close to this. I rarely experienced such in-depth conversations, even with my closest friends and family. Melanie penetrated this stranger's life with genuine interest and concern. I was stunned.

Usually it seems that most people don't listen well in conversations, but rather are simply waiting to talk. Most people typically find ways to make a conversation about them most of the time. I saw most people as competitive and generally disinterested in other people's lives, especially when it comes to those they don't know and have just met.

Melanie was genuinely interested in this person's life. An hour ago, she didn't know this person existed, and now she knew him shockingly well. She kept asking questions and listening intently, recalling things he had told us earlier in the conversation, which revealed how deeply engaged she was. She was making connections between different points in the conversation and expanding her understanding of his life.

A funny thing about it was this person knew practically nothing about Melanie or me. I don't recall that the server ever even asked who I was. I don't think I spoke the entire conversation, yet it was one of the most important conversations I was ever a part of, even though it was with a complete stranger.

Growing up in an ultrajudgmental, hypercritical environment, I believed people generally followed their own self-interests, put themselves first, and saw most others as opportunities, adversaries, or obstacles. I felt like people were always ready to pounce in any way they could and would try to make others look or feel stupid at every opportunity. That certainly wasn't the way Melanie saw the world around her, and she exuded an empathetic and compassionate spirit I didn't know existed in human beings. I'd never encountered anyone like her.

Melanie's spirit radiated as she relentlessly drove this one-sided conversation, digging ever deeper into the server's life. She was on the edge of her seat, leaning forward, fully engaged and intently focused on this person and his story. There was a gleam in her eye, a thrill in her voice, and joy in her laugh. It was obvious Melanie's appreciation of this guy was genuine. This wasn't an act. In the time I had spent with her, I had seen glimpses of this before, but I had no clue the extent of her compassion and the sincerity and genuineness with which she cared about other human beings—even ones she just met.

The conversation wasn't only for fun. She probed into his life with serious questions, and he opened up about challenges and frustrations with family and friends and other things to a degree that shocked me. My sense of awe grew. I was astounded.

I already had sensed that Melanie was a special person. The first signs of this had been her endless pack of friends. More materialized everywhere we went, and she'd always talk about other friends I hadn't met. Every time we went out with friends, new faces joined the core group. Not only were there a nearly uncountable number of friends, but they were all exceptionally fun and considerate. She surrounded herself with people who were a joy to be around, which was a wonderful reflection on the type of person she was. I had found this extraordinary person who was guiding me into a world that magnificently exceeded any expectations I had ever had for my life.

I knew it right then and there. I wanted this in my life—permanently. My heart opened to an incomprehensively authentic and extraordinary new world I didn't know existed. Until I met Melanie, I would have doubted it could exist, and yet I was now cradled in it. It was almost incomprehensible, yet so real. Our lunch encounter turned into one of the most significant moments of my life, so it had to be named. This was The Revelation of O'B Clark's, and with this revelation came the implied promise of an unimaginably wonderful and inspiring world filled with Melanie's radiant spirit of genuine caring, compassion, and kindness.

Melanie had no agenda that day. She wasn't trying to impress a boss or win a client's business. She was just Melanie being Melanie. It wasn't a ploy to impress me. I could have easily become jealous or annoyed because she wasn't focusing her attention on me. I'm proud that I had the good judgment to see this interaction for what it was and understand the significance of what it was revealing to me. It may sound pretentious or silly, but I sometimes think of myself as The Genius of O'B Clark's for how well I analyzed and interpreted this episode. I think it was the smartest thing I've ever done.

Melanie was so engaged in their conversation that she barely ate. I sat back and kept nibbling at the pizza until I ate most of it myself. And with that, here is the summation of the advice I would give to my kids, particularly my boys: If you ever meet a girl that you have boundless fun with, can talk to about anything, and you can laugh almost anywhere at any time, and then witness her projecting kindness when she has no need or reason to—and then you get to eat all the pizza on top of all that—put a ring on it.

I did.

I also left her a few pieces. It was a St. Louis–style pizza, which is thin crust. She liked the middle pieces with no extra crust at the edges. See, it's about knowing even the little things your friends or your partner likes and then being considerate of those things. Melanie always liked the middle pieces, so I always left those for her.

Several months later, I proposed to her. Looking back on it, I'm almost surprised it took several months. We discussed it during that time, and it was delayed as I was saving up money for a decent ring and all such traditions and protocols. But that day in O'B Clark's, after my revelation, I started opening up to her more than I ever had.

After the server finally left the scene, I told Melanie about the one skeleton in my closet that scared me, which to me felt like a dark secret that might just drive her away. Considering I was still somewhat the insecure and guilt-ridden kid that saw the world as hypercritical and ultrajudgmental, I feared she might see me as some deadbeat loser and not want to have anything to do with me any longer. I needed her to know this now so we could either dive deeper into this relationship or put an end to it.

I told her the story of the day I decided to apply to Parks College, and I left nothing out. I told her about waking up naked with my friend. I told her about the son that I might have in this world, that there was someone else involved, and there was a definite possibility that I was not the father. I found out she was pregnant on a phone call with a mutual friend, who was sharing news with me without realizing I might be involved. I was stunned, to say the least. I contemplated the whole thing for a while and then called my friend, the one who was pregnant.

She told me she had decided to have the baby but give it up for adoption. The adoption was already fully arranged and legally binding. I was broke and only beginning to attempt to turn my life around and make something out of it. Considering that the adoption was already arranged and I could barely take care of myself, I decided not to interfere. I don't remember when or how I found out, but I learned the child was a boy. The child was going to be adopted immediately by, from what I understood, a young couple who couldn't have children of their own. I was informed that they were well-educated professionals, which gave me the impression that the child would have a good home in at least those regards—far more than I could currently provide.

I told Melanie that while I didn't hide from it or deny anything, there were valid reasons to have doubts about the paternity. I willingly drove to Columbia, Missouri, from St. Louis to meet with the lawyer who arranged the adoption. They had listed me in all the legal documentation as the biological father. I explained to the lawyer my doubts and concerns. She seemed to understand even though she didn't seem to care. She just wanted me to sign where I needed to sign and move along. Perhaps I should have protested or insisted more on confirming paternity at that time, but the lawyer proceeded with me listed as the father without exhibiting much concern as to the truth of that declaration. I was still a young and naive boy barely learning to stand on his own two feet, so I signed without further protest.

However, I did make it clear to the lawyer that I wanted her to inform the adoptive parents personally and make sure it was noted in any documentation that I would be happy to be involved in any way they wanted. Further, if the child ever wanted to meet me some day, I was completely open to that, with one condition. Before taking any such steps, I wanted a paternity test to confirm that I was the biological father. I thought it would have been foolish and irresponsible not to do this. I did not want any of us to invest any time whatsoever in any such relationships unless we were certain that I was the child's father. After that meeting, I called my friend, the biological mother, and told her all this.

I felt this was the best I could do under my circumstances. I made it explicitly clear that I would be open and available at any point in time. DNA testing was still somewhat new in those days, but it had been commonly known for long enough that it was trusted and readily available. If the adoptive parents wanted me involved in any way, I was asking for the test first and then they would know where to find me. The biological mother and the lawyer knew where I lived and where my family lived, and it was legally documented. I would be easy to find. Years later, social media hit the scene, and I would be even easier to find. Despite my willingness to be involved, which was something I stated as clearly as I could, I never heard from anyone. In an unanticipated and indirect way, life would surprisingly provide the answer over a quarter of a century later.

On revelation day in O'B Clark's, I told Melanie things I had never told anyone else, and it scared me. She listened to the entire story intently and asked numerous questions. She never exhibited any reaction that even hinted of being critical or judgmental. She was supportive of me and my decisions and even offered some reassuring insights. I came out of it even a little glad that this young couple could now have a family of their own. I sincerely hoped they would be terrific parents to this child and raise him well and with lots of love, and I always continued to hope that I might eventually find out if he was actually my son. I came to consider that one person's poor decision can become someone else's blessing, and I hoped that was the result for this new family. I have thought about him every day of my life. Even if it would turn out he wasn't my son, I still wanted to know how he was and if he had a good life. I felt like I had a connection to him even if he wasn't my biological son.

My relationship with Melanie accelerated after that day. We saw each other even more frequently, and it was fantastic. We weren't uncomfortable in silent moments, but there weren't many silent moments. We could talk and laugh continuously. Her friends were amazing. My four friends and her 400 friends all became friends, and our world grew exponentially and thrived. I was having the time of my life. She continued to astound me with her kindness and random acts of compassion. She had an infectious smile and a contagious laugh that drew people to her. People gravitated to her, as she kept making new friends. She always made others the focal point while rarely talking about herself.

She once made a new friend in the tuna fish aisle at the grocery store. If I went into the tuna fish aisle, I would only expect to get out of the aisle with a couple of cans of tuna fish. Melanie comes out of the aisle with a new friend for life. We had dinner at the new friend's house two weeks later, and she's still a good friend to this day. In Melanie's world, this was not odd or unusual. She did the same thing in a parking lot one day. I was now living in a world of almost incomprehensible yet continuous acts of genuine kindness, compassion, and fun, until that world eventually became my new normal. After living so many years in a world I saw as hypercritical and ultrajudgmental, I later realized how blessed I was to live in the hyperfun and ultra-compassionate world of Melanie.

■ ■ ■ ■ ■ ■

I have one last tangent, for now. I feel compelled to explain why I'm sharing this story and writing this book, and there are many reasons. I believe in the power of sharing our stories. I don't believe that I'm some authority or expert full of wisdom that no one else possesses. I do believe that when people share their stories honestly and candidly, we help one another. It bolsters us and empowers us to know we aren't alone in things, to know that others have suffered yet survived and thrived and prospered. It gives us perspective and context in our own lives, but the teller of a story must be exhaustively candid to be truly powerful and beneficial. The teller must share things that aren't fun to share, to reveal things no one wants to reveal, regardless of how humbling it might be to do. It's a scary thing to do—terrifying—inviting criticism and ridicule, not to mention reliving the worst moments of life in excruciating detail, but sometimes that is how we answer the call to help one another and make this world a better place. I used to be afraid of everything, but not so much anymore. I'm letting it all out.

I remember being in Boy Scouts as a kid and going on a camping trip. When we set up camp, our troop leader gathered us together and gave us a little speech. One of things he said was that we should leave our campsite a little nicer and a little cleaner than we'd found it. His words hit me, and I've never forgotten them. I sometimes think it's funny that, at some point, that camp leader probably thought the kids never listened to him, yet here I am over four decades later recounting his words that I've never forgotten. What we say and do often has a far greater impact than we're ever aware of, both positively and negatively, and kids pick up on—and remember—a lot more than we think.

I know I did because I remember being struck, even as a young kid, by the significance of those words, and I realized how those words applied to all of life. I've tried to live by them, and it remains a goal of mine. I want to leave this world and this life at least a little better than it was when I came into it. I feel compelled to answer that call, and that's a phrase that constantly comes to mind: "answer the call." I feel like one way to answer that call is to tell this story, to write this book as candidly as I can. I desperately want to answer the call and feel I left this world with something positive and useful.

If I can get this book written and published, I'll feel I did my best to answer the call, even if hardly anyone ever reads it. I've learned to only concern myself with the things I can control. I can control writing this and publishing it. I can't control who reads it, so I'll focus on answering the call to put it out there.

Another reason for telling this story is that I want our kids to know things about their mom, who she was, and what she was like. I want to share life lessons I've learned with our kids and leave it all in print so that they and the generations who follow will have this information. And not just our kids—I want the world to know about Melanie. She was a rare and beautiful spirit who opened my eyes to all the best of this world and all the best of people.

Since Melanie's mom died when she was only nine, she wanted to learn more about her mom as she got older. Melanie's lone sibling, Stephanie, was only 12 when their mom passed. As adults, they asked their uncle what their mom was like and to share stories about her. Their uncle told them that when their mom was getting ready to go to college, she was heavy, and they all told her that she needed to lose weight if she wanted to have any fun in college. That was the only thing he shared with them about their mother, his sister.

Enlightening.

I'd like to leave our children with just a little more information about their mom, maybe just a little bit more.

■ ■ ■ ■ ■ ■

So now I'm *finally* done with the backstories to the backstory and the tangents to those backstories. You're welcome.

4

Toughness Defined

Back in that emergency room, it didn't surprise me in the slightest to watch Melanie interrogate Martin and Kelly. It remained impressive and endearing, which was why I was still in awe of her after more than 21 years together and nearly 19 years of marriage. It was perfectly in character for Melanie. She put others first and cherished every relationship, and now did so despite the fact that she was the one having a potentially life-threatening stroke caused by her cancer. She could barely form her words, and yet there she was digging into Martin and Kelly's life and putting them first, which they found extraordinary. Living with Melanie, this extraordinary had become my ordinary.

Her speech kept improving, and everything else was stable. Within the next hour or so, they moved her out of the emergency room to a regular patient room upstairs. I still couldn't find my phone. Since Martin and Kelly were with her, I was going to run to my car and then meet them in the new room. When I reached into my pocket for my car keys, I couldn't find them either, then I discovered I didn't have my wallet either. I mentioned this to Martin, and the nurse overheard me.

"You probably left it all at security," she said. The way she said it, I got the feeling that this happened all the time. "People do it all the time," the nurse confirmed. As they all started off to her new room, I went back to security.

"I wondered when you'd be back," the security guard said. I collected my stuff and headed upstairs quickly.

By the time I got there, Melanie's speech had noticeably improved. She seemed in better spirits. The room was tiny. It was probably the smallest hospital room I'd ever been in, and yet it was double occupancy. Another patient was in the other bed with a few family members visiting. Despite a curtain being drawn between us, the beds were probably only a couple feet apart, and we felt like we were sitting in the laps of the other family. It made the room quite loud. Martin and Kelly stayed for a bit and then headed home.

Melanie and I talked, and I even had her smiling and laughing a little. I don't remember what she said, but she finally said a short but complete sentence, enunciating every word clearly and without hesitation. It was her first complete sentence in hours, and she realized it immediately.

"A-HA!" she cackled. Her eyes lit up and she pointed at me with a look of joyous triumph as her lips formed a victorious smile. She was fighting her way back as she had been doing all along.

"*Suck it, Trebek!*" she exclaimed, also perfectly spoken, laughing with a huge smile at her expression of one of our little pet phrases. It came from a skit on *Saturday Night Live* called Celebrity Jeopardy. An impersonator of Sean Connery would say obnoxious and crude things throughout the show, annoying the Alex Trebek character, the host of the show. At some point in the skit, the Sean Connery character says, "Suck it, Trebek," and Melanie and I thought that was hilarious. We immediately adopted it as a catch-all phrase, expressing anything depending on the context of when and how it was said. It could be to hurl an insult, indicate surprise, convey approval, dictate a command, validate victory in an argument, or express dozens of other emotions or thoughts.

"Suck it, Trebek!" I echoed right back at her with a proud smile.

She was back. This was going to be just another bump in the road, like numerous other ones she'd overcome. As we talked, her speech continued to improve rapidly and soon was almost perfect again. We were having an ordinary conversation, like thousands of other conversations we'd been having for more than two decades. We were momentarily oblivious to the other patient and visitors behind the curtain, despite being only a few feet away. Our little victory had us elated.

A hospital staffer brought in a tray of food. Concerns about these clots and strokes and her vision issues lingered in my mind, but I basked in the momentary relief and felt confident we could deal with it now that we knew what we were dealing with and the doctors were on it.

"I can't believe you made me get you different pants," I said, and she smiled.

"Those ones you got get all itchy," she explained.

I smiled and shook my head a little but let that one go.

"I meeean...*cominee*?" Melanie said. "What was that word? What was I even saying?"

"I don't know..." I thought about it, considering the sounds in that word. It struck me that she remembered saying that and what it revealed about her cognitive abilities throughout the episode, but I didn't dwell on it. "Maybe you were trying to say, 'Come and get me'?"

"Maybe!" She laughed a little. "I bet that's it!"

Melanie wanted to eat, which was a good sign. The tray contained a sandwich, a cup of applesauce, and a couple other items. She asked for the applesauce. I stepped around the bed to where the food was and pulled the foil cover off the cup.

"It's starting to feel like it did before," Melanie said.

For a couple seconds, what she said refused to register in my mind. She was looking down at her right forearm and stroking it with her left hand, as she had when sitting on the sofa at our house. A tidal wave of panic swelled up within me, but I also had the sense to keep my composure and not cause fear and panic in her.

"What do you mean?" I asked in a carefully measured tone.

"Like when I was in the shower," she said.

Every cuss word I know fired off in my head in unison. I watched her intently. The expression on her face changed abruptly, and the fear was evident.

"I'll call the nurse," I said.

Before I could move, she started trying to speak, but only a garbled stream of gibberish came out. I hit the call button for the nurse, screaming a thousand thoughts in my head. This couldn't be happening, not again.

"I'm going to see if a nurse or doctor is nearby," I told her. I didn't want to wait around, relying on the call button. She needed someone immediately. *I* needed someone with her immediately.

I bolted out the door and charged down the hallway, frantically looking for anyone. I saw no one. I didn't want to get far from Melanie. I was aware it was late, and I didn't want to disturb other patients who needed rest, but this was a hospital and this was an emergency, and despite retaining some situational awareness, I'm sure I wasn't thinking clearly overall.

I yelled out that we needed a nurse or a doctor and shouted the room number, and then I ran back to Melanie. I didn't want her to be alone. Between my bellowing and the call button, someone should be alerted to us and our need. I told Melanie someone would be here soon and tried to say reassuring things to her. I don't remember what I said, but I kept talking to her. I didn't have to talk for long. Her nurse was back in the room quickly, and I maneuvered out of the way as best I could in the tiny room.

The nurse began asking her questions, but now Melanie could not speak at all, not even the gibberish. The nurse stepped her through the tongue and eyebrow exercises. I felt confident the nurse was doing all the best she could, but it was again frustrating that she wasn't doing more. There were no shots or treatments being given to stop what was happening. The nurse was mostly observing her.

"So, what's happening to her?" I finally asked when the nurse paused.

The nurse gave me some answer that didn't really sound like an answer.

"Is she having another stroke?" I asked pointedly.

"No, she's not showing signs of another stroke," the nurse answered without further explanation.

We were told by multiple doctors and nurses that what happened to Melanie at home was a stroke. What was happening to her now seemed nearly identical to what Melanie experienced before, but now this nurse was saying this was not a stroke. I was confused, frustrated, and terrified, to say the least. She had recovered from her stroke and had been speaking perfectly again, so what was happening now? Was this some poststroke episode, like an aftershock following an earthquake?

"If this isn't a stroke," I asked the nurse, "then what is happening to her?"

The nurse gave another answer I didn't understand. Everything about this frightened me, and the nurse's inability to explain what was happening was exasperating. Was this some other kind of episode, something worse than a stroke? So many questions; no answers.

I asked more questions, desperately trying to understand what was happening. The nurse was getting slightly annoyed with the questions. She finally had me join her in front of Melanie and instructed her to do the tongue and eyebrow exercises. She pointed out to me how Melanie's cheeks and eyebrows went up evenly and other observations that indicated another stroke was unlikely. I was bewildered and terrified. She was having an episode seemingly identical to the stroke she just had, but it wasn't a stroke? What was it? I was back to fearing the cancer spread into her brain. What were we dealing with, and how would we get past it?

Another staffer came into the room, stating that they would be moving Melanie to another area where she could get additional attention. I was glad something was being done. They wasted no time, and we were on our way down the hall in minutes. I had no objections to leaving that cramped room and that confounding nurse. We took the elevator to another floor. The other staffer was pushing Melanie and talking along the way. Once we got settled in the new room, she told Melanie's new nurse a few things and then disappeared.

Our new nurse got Melanie situated in her new bed, with all the proper wires and tubes and gadgets in the right places. Although this was another double-occupancy room, it was far bigger than the last one. Melanie did have a roommate, who was asleep with no visitors. It was much more peaceful and comfortable than the previous room, other than the usual beeps and buzzes and dings and hisses and hums of the various monitors and gadgets. Melanie was exhausted and fell asleep during this process, but the nurse woke her once she had everything arranged to do her own evaluation. We immediately liked this nurse. She had a terrific personality and demeanor. Melanie gave me her customary nod of approval. She asked Melanie many of the same questions and instructed her to perform the tongue and eyebrow exercises. The nurse stayed in the room for a surprisingly long time, and we learned that she was assigned only to this room, not doing rounds across the entire floor or multiple rooms. She was dedicated to Melanie.

When she finished her tasks, I asked her if this was a stroke or some other kind of episode, but again the answers weren't helpful. Her attitude was terrific. She seemed genuinely sorry that she couldn't answer my questions more definitively, courteously advising me it might be better for me to speak with the doctor. However, she wasn't sure when the floor doctor would be coming by. While I was still frustrated that no one could explain what was happening in a way I could understand, I appreciated this nurse's attitude, and our interactions remained amicable.

When I looked at my watch, it was past midnight, which was much later than I'd thought. Melanie was exhausted and fell asleep while I was talking to the nurse. Although it was incredibly hard to leave, we had discussed keeping daily life as normal and routine for the kids as possible. The kids were at home with Melanie's sister, who texted me earlier when she brought them back to our house and put them to bed.

When I got home, Stephanie and her daughter were asleep on our sofa, and all my kids were sound asleep. I barely slept the entire night. I may have dozed off a few times and drifted in and out of some strange, dreamlike states. In one, I heard a doctor tell me Melanie had passed away, and I jolted up in bed barely able to breathe. My mind raced, wondering if Melanie was having another of these episodes that no one could explain. Once again, I couldn't shake the feeling that I was not going to see her alive again. I kept waiting for the phone to ring, expecting a call notifying me that Melanie had had another massive, undefined episode and had passed. It was a long night, and finally the bedroom curtains began to glow as the morning sun illuminated them. The room filled with light. I continued to lay in bed, staring at Melanie's clothes and other possessions and wondering.

I don't recall when Stephanie and her daughter left. I can't even remember if I spoke to them or if they just slipped out early. The next thing I remember was a bedroom door opening and one of my kids coming into my room and into my bed. The child lay sideways across the bed facing away from me.

"Daddy..."

"Yes?" I said.

"I had a dream that mommy was sleeping with her eyes open and I couldn't wake her up."

An overpowering burst of emotion surged through me with an immediacy I have never felt before, as if every atom in my body was splitting simultaneously.

Why was this child having this dream on this night? Was this some sort of mother-child telepathy or clairvoyance, or worse? Had Melanie's spirit departed her body in death and visited the child during the night? These thoughts and a thousand others screamed out in my head. I am not a believer in ghosts and such things, and yet

I was consumed with the thought that Melanie had passed away and channeled into our child. I suddenly believed in ghosts, or something of the kind.

This instant internal emotional explosion was unlike anything else I have ever experienced. I felt completely powerless to contain it in any way, and yet, somehow, I managed to only make one short gasping noise that involuntarily burst from me. I somehow managed to fake a cough, fighting to mask that gasp to prevent frightening our child.

"It was just a dream," I said, not sure I believed my own words. I don't know how I managed to think or verbalize them. If this child had been facing me and looking at me, I don't think I could have kept it together as I did.

"Mommy is okay. She's with the doctors still, and they're taking care of her," I told the child, feeling as if I was telling a lie. I gave the child a hug from behind. "Let's get some breakfast."

We headed out of the bedroom. I turned on the lights to the kids' bedrooms and called them to wake up. I was internally screaming in horror, shaking in terror on the inside, yet externally managing to get the kids ready as if this was a normal morning. They didn't seem to notice anything unusual in my behavior, so I guess I was somehow keeping it together, at least on the outside.

"Where's mom?" one of the other kids asked when coming down the hall.

"The doctors wanted to keep her there a little longer and check some more things on her." They were accustomed to her hospital stays and knew she had been there for the last few days. They thought she was coming home yesterday, but my answer was enough for them. As the next two children made their way down the hall, each asked the same question and got the same answer.

The kids went through their stages of eating and getting dressed. I put lunches together and then went back into my bedroom to get dressed myself. My phone dinged with an incoming text message. I was afraid to read it, but I realized the doctors would be calling, not texting, if they had news.

"Bring a fountain please." The sender was Melanie. I fell back on the bed. She was alive. She was communicating. It was the single greatest text message I had ever received.

Suck it, Trebek!

Family and friends had graciously offered to drive the kids to their various schools, so I finished getting them ready and shuffled them out to their rides as the vehicles arrived. I grabbed some additional items for Melanie and headed back to the hospital. When I arrived, she was sitting up with the back of the bed raised, and the same nurse from last night was still attending to her. The nurses worked 12-hour shifts, and they hadn't changed shifts yet.

Melanie's speech was decent but not as good as it had been. The nurse informed me she had had another episode overnight. I wanted to ask again what these episodes were, but I didn't bother since I'd already asked this nurse the night before.

"The doctor will be making rounds this morning," the nurse informed me, as if reading my mind. "She should come by in the next hour or so."

The nurse left the room. I had already noticed that the other bed was empty. The roommate was likely out for tests or treatment, as there were personal items on that side of the room beyond the curtain. Melanie and I talked a little, and while her speech was broken and strained, she could communicate clearly enough for me to understand her. She asked for something from one of her bags and a couple other comfort requests. After I obliged, she scooted up in the bed closer to me and leaned forward, sitting up on her own. We were silent for a few moments.

"Am I going to die?"

I didn't want to pause on that one too long, and luckily an answer came to mind quickly.

"Someday," I said, "but not anytime soon." Despite multiple recent instances of my own panicked feelings that I wouldn't see Melanie again, I believed this when I said it to her. It made me feel better to say it, as if being able to verbalize it made it true. "The doctors are on this. You'll get the care you need, and they'll figure it out." I squeezed her hand and kissed her on the forehead.

After a brief pause, Melanie looked me in the eye intently. "When I'm gone, you need to find a new wife," she said sternly. Melanie had told me this at least a couple times before, most notably after her initial diagnosis and again after she was diagnosed with the liver tumor. When she said it this time, the words carried a far greater order of magnitude.

Despite the magnitude, I really wanted to tell her to shut up. This wasn't a path I wanted to consider. It wasn't something I wanted to think about, not now and, really, not ever. Among its many little perks, cancer triggers odd and uncomfortable conversations you never would have expected to have. I blinked once slowly and gave the subtlest motion of a nod, which was the quickest and most placid way I could both acknowledge and dismiss her proclamation.

She wasn't accepting my dismissal. Melanie knew my history and my yearnings—and my lack thereof. I didn't meet Melanie until I was a few weeks shy of my 29th birthday. I wasn't some young naive kid jumping into the first decent relationship that presented itself. I had dated my fair share, but I had never dated anyone for more than two months before I met her. I'm about as opposite of codependent as they come. While I'm tolerant and accepting of people and even really enjoy friendships, even the more casual ones, I couldn't get in deeper with someone if I didn't see a future there. I'm not afraid of commitment. I dove right in with Melanie when I saw that future, and I genuinely believe having a committed relationship is the overall best way for us to live. However, I always believed that getting involved with someone without the right fit is a recipe for disaster. It's hard enough to make a committed relationship work when it's a good fit, and it always sounded miserable to me to dedicate my life to someone who wasn't an excellent fit. If I didn't see a longer path, I would end a relationship outright.

Melanie knew all this, and she knew it well. We would laugh about it. In a sitcom we used to watch centered on a married couple, a friend of theirs had an affair in one episode. As the husband and wife discussed the affair, they discussed how the husband sometimes got a little jealous and concerned when she flirted with other men, but then the wife expressed absolutely no concern about the husband ever having an affair. He was offended by this. He took it as if she thought he wasn't attractive enough or charming enough or didn't have the skills to flirt successfully with other woman, as if he didn't have game. But the wife then comically explains that she knows he's too lazy and too easily annoyed. She says he couldn't handle the time and effort to arrange all the secret rendezvous. Melanie laughed hysterically at that and said that was exactly me, and I laughed right along with her, knowing it was true. I couldn't imagine living my days worrying about getting caught and feeling guilty about it all.

Lots of people do it, and I don't think I'm better than them. I'm just too lazy, and it sounds like a miserable way to live life to me.

When I tried to dismiss Melanie's edict, she looked me even more intensely in the eye and spoke deliberately, though she struggled with the words. "You need someone to take care of you, and the kids need a mom."

She cast her eyes down on those last words and dropped her face into her hands. "The kids," she said. "How would the kids even handle that?" Melanie looked as distraught as I had ever seen her. This thought seemed to overwhelm her.

That was an easy answer for me. I didn't hesitate.

"We got Kesem." I said this matter-of-factly, as if it were so obvious that I couldn't believe she hadn't thought of it. I even shrugged as I said it.

Camp Kesem is not just a camp, as I think of it. I consider it more of a community: a child's friend through and beyond a parent's cancer. Melanie learned about it and got our oldest kids registered within months of her diagnosis. It is the most outstanding organization I have ever encountered. They run a weeklong overnight summer camp and then various activities throughout the year. It's operated out of colleges. They had over 100 chapters when we first joined and have grown every year. We were in the St. Louis University chapter. The counselors are all college students, and they are the greatest role models I've ever encountered—by far. One lesson I've learned in life is how critical it is to identify the good resources available and utilize those resources. I can't quantify or qualify what a monumental difference Camp Kesem has made in our world throughout our entire cancer journey and beyond.

"We do have Kesem," Melanie said, and I could see much of the fear and distress quickly drain back out of her. "I'm so grateful we found them. What a blessing."

What can you say about an organization so extraordinary that it can melt away some of a mother's worst fears, including the imminent end of her own life and her time with her children? Whenever I deal with Camp Kesem or even think about it, I continue to be amazed by how awesome they are and, almost incomprehensively, that they really do exist. Camp Kesem, like Melanie herself, revealed things more wonderful than I used to believe could actually exist in this world.

"You know," I said, now thinking more about the kids, "I'm going to have to talk to the kids about your condition. We need to prepare them for how you'll be talking and that they need to help around the house more and how you'll need help." I had been dreading this discussion, but it was time. We had to be on the same page on this one.

"Yeah, lucky you," Melanie said. It was exactly the kind of comment I would expect from her. She was an exceptionally kind and caring person, but she wasn't fake or rah-rah positive. She had an amazing ability to deal with things in a real way, and sarcasm was one of her favorite tools. "You get to go home and tell the kids what a freak their mom has become. You're welcome."

Before I could even begin to think of a response to that, her face scrunched together and she exploded into tears, as did I. I jumped up from the chair and threw my arms around her, as raw emotion poured from us. I laid my cheek on her bald head, and we continued to cry uncontrollably for several minutes. In fifty years of life, I had never cried like that—not that hard and never for anywhere near that long. Later, I would try to think of what I had said to her during this eruption, but I realized I had not said anything. I'd been incapable of saying anything. I may have blurted out the words, "I love you," once or twice, but they may not have been audible.

It was painful. I had no idea until then how much crying can physically hurt. My eyes burned, and I got a splitting headache. What's fascinating to me, as I reflect on this moment, is the conflict and the contradiction between how I would try to control my feelings and what I really needed from my feelings. I was fighting against the crying the entire time. I hated it and struggled to make it stop. Yet, looking back, I'm grateful for it. Although I couldn't stand it at the time, it may have been the most telling single moment of our life together. That absolutely and unconditionally pure, visceral expression of the love we shared could never be expressed in words. I couldn't fake or even embellish a moment like that, and I'm eternally grateful for it.

When we regained our composure, we had a few rare minutes of silence, until the next wave of doctors, nurses, specialists, and technicians paraded through. They ran numerous speech and motion tests, each one repeating many of the same questions and requests but with some unique directives. One of them was a therapist, and she explained that while some of these tests were only for evaluation purposes, others were therapeutic and could help Melanie regain and improve her speech.

Melanie and I were immediately on the same page on that one. As Melanie started to tell me to write those down, I was already digging pen and paper out of a bag. We had the therapist go back over those questions and exercises, and I wrote them all down. The therapist confirmed that it would help to practice more on her own and not wait for the therapists. Now we knew what to practice.

The parade of different medical professionals making their rounds continued after the therapist left, and Melanie looked exhausted when we finally got a break. I expected her to nap, but she surprised me when she asked to do the exercises again. The therapist had explained that Melanie could get her speech mostly, perhaps even completely, back to normal, but there were no guarantees, and it could take months or even up to a year. Nevertheless, now that Melanie understood that possibility, she was determined to get her speech back. She wasn't wasting any time.

I was proud of her and impressed. What a fighter. What strength. Not much earlier, she was asking me if she was going to die and planning contingencies for her family after her death, and yet despite her fears, she was determined to battle back. The exercises ranged from relatively easy to difficult and frustrating, but even the relatively easy ones were challenging with her speech compromised. She would answer questions like where she lived or how old she was, which were the easiest. Then there were things like reciting lists. She would recite the names of her kids from youngest to oldest, then reverse the order from oldest to youngest. Then she would recite their ages, and then she would say each name and age together, and then reverse the order. There were numerous such exercises, and they became more difficult. I tried a couple of the harder ones, and they were difficult for me to do, which made her feel better about not being able to do those much at all. At times, she grew frustrated and even cried a little when struggling on some parts, but she didn't quit and fought through the entire practice list.

Then she really stunned me. When she finished the list and I started to set it down, she said, "Again." She pointed at the list and then rolled her hand in a circular motion like she was telling me to crank it up. I was surprised by her determination, her strength, her dedication, and her persistence. She went through the entire practice list again, struggling through much of it but never stopping. There was no quit in her.

And then finally, looking extremely exhausted, she dozed off for a bit.

I spent some time alternating from her phone to mine answering copious text messages. The news about Melanie had spread quickly. It was late morning now, and the nurses had just completed shift change. Once they finished their briefings and the overnight nurse left, I asked the new nurse about the episodes. While also courteous and professional, she wasn't able to provide an explanation that helped me understand. Melanie woke up once and spoke briefly to the new nurse, and then she fell back asleep. I kept processing the onslaught of text messages. I learned to write updates as generically as possible, without anything specific to a particular individual, so I could copy and paste a given message to others. The generic messages weren't sufficient much of the time, so I still had to write specifically modified responses, but this approach saved time and effort.

After a while, the roommate was brought back in. I spoke to her briefly, learning that her name was Sylvia. She was kind, and I liked her immediately, but her crass language and demeanor gave the impression that she'd had a hard life. Her son came in for a few minutes. He didn't seem to be a pleasant person. He didn't stay long. I wouldn't miss him.

Melanie was awoken by another parade of hospital workers. When they finally disappeared, she looked exhausted and I expected her to fall asleep. She settled back onto her pillows and closed her eyes.

"That your wife?" Sylvia asked quietly.

I nodded. I was sitting at the tail end of the curtain near the foot of the bed, so I could easily look around the curtain and see Sylvia.

"Wait!" Melanie's eyes popped open. "*Who's that?*"

"Sylvia." I chuckled. "Your roommate."

"Well, hel-lo *Sylvia*!" Even with her speech impaired, Melanie's exclamation was understandable and enthusiastic.

"Hey there!" Sylvia responded.

"Pull…!" Melanie looked at me and waved her hand at the obstructing curtain. She had to meet Sylvia. That was Melanie, always pulling back the curtains. What a perfect metaphor for her life.

Before I even started drawing the curtain back, Melanie launched into an interrogation of Sylvia, and Sylvia was patient and considerate of Melanie's speech. I thought of The Revelation of O'B Clark's where I saw how I would live in this world of genuine caring and compassion with this phenomenal woman, and how often I'd seen it over the years.

■■■■■■

As I watched this latest interrogation commence, I was reminded of one of the most remarkable instances of Melanie I'd ever experienced. It was about two years earlier. Melanie and I were on the sofa in our living room watching television when the phone rang. As she answered, I paused the show. The conversation instantly was friendly, and Melanie, as usual, was firing questions at whoever was on the other end of the line. Melanie had many friends, and such calls were so common that I had developed a game to guess who was on the other end of the line and see how fast I could figure it out.

This caller was a mom with a kid who had just started driving, which eliminated many possible friends. They talked about the caller's husband and a lot of other personal things that I sort of heard but halfway zoned out. The call went on for at least fifteen minutes, covering all sorts of personal chit-chat that could have revealed the identity of the caller, but this one had me stumped. It became apparent the call was not going to end quickly, so I went over to my computer to check email and headlines. I gave up, figuring this was likely a new friend I didn't know, which happened frequently with Melanie.

"Who was that?" I asked when she hung up. And then I did what husbands everywhere do every day—I started to zone out and not really listen to her response.

She said something about it being so-and-so from such-and-such. I didn't recognize the person's name, but the company name caught my limited zoned-out attention and made me curious. Based on the name of the company, I was immediately struck by the notion that something didn't add up about this. Why would Melanie be talking so personally to someone from such a place?

"What is that company?"

Melanie told me what company it was, which only confused me more. I thought about it for a few moments.

"Wait…so…have you become friends with the *bill collector*?"

"Well…yeah. I mean, she calls here every week," Melanie explained. "What I am supposed to do, be rude to her?"

"Well, yeah—" I started to say but stopped. Even for me, knowing Melanie as well as I did, this one just didn't want to sink in.

I felt I needed to explain to Melanie that *normal* human behavior is to be rude to bill collectors. People screen their calls, argue with them, yell at them, and call them all sorts of nasty things. What *nobody* does—what I wouldn't have imagined was possible and never expected even after years of knowing Melanie—was befriend a bill collector, and over the phone. I meeean...*who does that*?

Melanie. Only Melanie.

This was the extraordinary world I had come to live in. The realization of that unspoken promise in The Revelation of O'B Clark's—that if I built a life with Melanie, I would live in a world where genuine caring and extraordinary compassion was the norm—had become my reality, but this one shocked me, even after years of watching Melanie be Melanie.

She remained that way consistently, even throughout our hard times. Hard times can change people. Hard times can end marriages and destroy relationships. Melanie and I had been through plenty of hard times. A few years earlier, we invested nearly every dollar we had into a business I started with partners. The wealthy partners invested a tiny fraction of their worth, and they weren't involved in the daily work. For us, putting in our share left us broke.

I architected and engineered a complex software system, what's called an enterprise resource management system. With the help of an outsourced development resource, we coded the entire system and had it ready to deploy in record time. Multiple people had told me this couldn't be done and that I was crazy, but I believed it and I did it. It was an amazing accomplishment and a tremendous source of pride. I am a huge believer in the importance of accomplishments, and this was one of my greatest personal and professional accomplishments.

One of the partners was supposed be our salesman, but he did an awful job. He didn't understand the industry or technology, and he kept practically giving the system away because he didn't believe customers would pay. He thought we needed more references to prove it worked, and hubris prevented him from considering any other possibility. As much as I believe in kindness and compassion and value people, business is business—and business is about money. Without money, you can't produce anything. And if you can't produce, you can't help anyone. Avarice is a vice, but continually giving your product away is just plain stupidity.

We couldn't keep up with the work required to implement and support the system for the clients we had, and they were barely paying for it. My decision to change things and the action I took solved the issue, but it was also the catalyst for the beginning of the end of our company. I came up with an alternative, viable sales strategy and took over sales responsibilities. While my strategy had multiple elements to it, the ingenious core element was to charge actual money for the system. This wasn't rocket science or brain surgery. I effectively ousted the other partner from that role, which apparently was a huge—no, gargantuan—hit to his inflated ego.

In a market where competing systems were selling for $300,000 and up, he had sold the system to nine clients for a *combined* total of $16,000 over three years, with no significant sales on the horizon. We were hemorrhaging the money we had invested. Within three months of taking over sales, I landed a *single* sale of over $65,000. We had a check in hand. We were a startup on a shoestring budget, and we needed approximately $200,000 in new revenue to cover operating expenses for the next year. After about four years of development, we were finally on a viable path to becoming profitable, and everything was in place to do it.

While I was landing that sale and cultivating others, the partners were meeting behind my back and elected to exercise a clause to shut down the company. It was over. They had the lawyer send me a letter a week before Christmas terminating the entire operation. They didn't even have the decency or the guts to tell me themselves. I never spoke to them again. Since I never spoke to them again, I don't know to this day if they know that three weeks later one of my prospective clients called me on my personal cell phone, frustrated because they had been trying to contact us and no one was responding to them. I no longer had access to company email or phones. The client had decided to buy our system and was excited about it. They had signed the contract and were ready to send in a check for $108,000. We had made over $170,000 in a little over three months. With one more sale in that price range within the next several months, we would have been profitable for the year. We'd made it and were now a profitable operation on a monthly basis—except we were shut down.

I learned an amazing lesson: sometimes you make it without making it. Sometimes people make incredibly bad decisions when their egos get in the way. It is incomprehensible to me on so many levels, but it happened.

However, it turned out to be a blessing in disguise. I landed a great job within weeks. Melanie got diagnosed with Wegener's months later and then got her cancer diagnosis the next year. Our startup company had horrible insurance, and Melanie would accrue at least two million dollars in medical expenses over the next four years. The excellent insurance at the company where I landed covered practically all of that. More importantly, the success our startup could have had would have required excessive time over the coming years to build the company, and I wouldn't have been able to be there as much with Melanie through her treatments and surgeries. Sometimes you make it without making it, and sometimes it's the best thing for you.

When the business went down, Melanie and I were effectively bankrupt. At one point, I had $3.17 in my checking account, with four kids to feed, including a newborn. Fortunately, I had found a job quickly. We never declared bankruptcy legally, but we were close. We had a stack of unpaid and past due bills that was always on our table. Failing to find a more creative name, I simply called this The Stack. The Stack mocked me daily, taunting me over the failure of the business. When the bill collector, Melanie's friend, called that evening, The Stack was there mocking me, even though we'd managed to keep up with things overall. The collection agency was calling on a bill of only about $250, and—believe it or not—the reason we hadn't paid it was Melanie.

Melanie had been misdiagnosed at a local hospital by a rude technician who had upset Melanie tremendously. The technician overstepped her bounds by even discussing a diagnosis with a patient, giving Melanie erroneous information in doing so. Melanie didn't trust the technician or that hospital and had doubts about the diagnosis, which originally went from not being cancer to being cancer, with some highly questionable explanations and backtracking along the way. Melanie consulted with her cousin David, a doctor, and after getting his advice and recommendations, she went to the Siteman Cancer Center in St. Louis and got tested there. The original hospital, despite their misdiagnosis of life-threatening breast cancer, still billed us about $250 for their services, which Melanie refused to pay.

And refused to pay. And refused to pay.

For over three years, Melanie refused to pay that $250, and the hospital sent it to a collection agency. While I have explained how extraordinary Melanie is and how much I could be in awe of her, I won't give a false narrative and claim she was some perfect person.

She could be as stubborn and hardheaded as anyone I have ever known, and her temper could explode without notice. I can't even tell you how many times I heard the doors of our kitchen cabinets slammed shut over the years; just thinking about that sound makes me cringe.

But her upside was nearly incomprehensible and unimaginable. When I learned that she had befriended the bill collector and I started to think of how I needed to explain to her that this was not normal human behavior, I was struck simultaneously by two thoughts. The first thought was to not bother, as if I were going to change her. The second thought was why would I want to change her? This unusual friendship was almost unacceptably odd at first, but what was so wrong with it? It was extraordinary. It was uniquely Melanie. It was even better than what I had envisioned or hoped for that day in O'B Clark's.

■■■■■■

On that day in the hospital when Melanie began her interrogation of Sylvia, I wasn't the slightest bit surprised. Nothing, not cancer, not strokes, not surgeries, not speech impairment, and not even fear of death could keep Melanie from being Melanie. She struggled at times to form her words, and sometimes I would help when I understood what she was asking. Their conversation was almost exclusively Melanie asking about Sylvia and Sylvia talking about her life and family.

Nurses and other staff came in for both patients, and sometimes they had to pause the conversation and sometimes not. Sometimes the nurses or staff members got involved in the conversation. A few times, the nurses closed the curtain for privacy, but as soon as they completed their tasks, Melanie would have me pulling back the curtain again. They talked for hours. Once again, I was back in O'B Clark's. Once again, the conversation was primarily one-sided. Melanie had Sylvia talking about her kids, her husband, her job, her friends, television shows, and even her childhood. Sylvia must have been 70 years old, and Melanie had her talking about her childhood for twenty minutes. I appreciated this at the time. I felt impressed by and proud of Melanie. Once again, I was in awe of her.

We all want to be tough, at least in some way. I realized years ago that there are many types of toughness. As a dumb young guy, I thought toughness was primarily a physical trait. While physical toughness can be more apparent, I've found mental and emotional toughness are typically more beneficial and more frequently needed. I've learned that no one is tough in every way. I've struggled to determine what kind of tough I really wanted or needed to be. I couldn't identify it or define it. When I reflected on that day in the hospital, I realized that Melanie provided me with yet another revelation by showing me that the greatest manifestation of toughness is kindness.

Some may scoff at that notion. It might sound like a contradiction in terms. As I've thought about it, I realized that it is easy to lash out at someone in frustration. It is far easier to lose your cool than to hold it together. It is far easier to quit than to keep going. Such actions reveal weakness. I was astounded to realize how tough it is to rise to the next level and project kindness on others when you have every reason to lose it. That's toughness defined.

Earlier that day, Melanie was asking if she was going to die. She was suffering through more ominous mystery episodes that teams of medical experts couldn't explain to us. She was fearing for her kids and facing an increased likelihood that she would not be around to see them grow up. She fought through frustrations in speech exercises and stayed strong. If I have ever witnessed someone who had more justification for wallowing in self-pity and breaking down and lashing out at another, Melanie was there that day. The fears had been building for years, and it felt as if the end might finally be drawing near. I couldn't have blamed her if she just railed on someone, or at least disregarded them and focused on herself.

In the bed next to Melanie was a woman who many people would have disregarded. Yet Melanie, in her own worst hours, put this woman on a pedestal and treated her like a queen. She showed Sylvia respect and compassion and friendship. On a day when I couldn't have blamed Melanie for exhibiting the worst of behaviors, she instead rose to an unprecedented level and showed the strength of spirit to exhibit unbridled kindness in the most severely disheartening moments of her own life.

She showed me the kind of man I want to be. She showed me the kind of person I want to be. She showed me the kind of human being I want to be. In that moment, I was watching a hard-core badass battling her greatest fears, wearing the armor of benevolence and leading the way to show me the light—to show us all the light. She was a survivor. She was a fighter. She was a warrior. As such, she is a portrait of hope for us all. She is the standard. She is a role model for us all. She is an example of the greatest level we can attain as human beings, and she should be immortalized.

This woman, bald from chemotherapy with significantly impaired speech, showed me things more than extraordinary in a moment that was less than ordinary. Even more important, she taught me that the extraordinary is in the ordinary all around me, and she showed me how to find it.

5

The Chemo Party

The next day started much like the previous day, except I was lucky enough not to hear any terror-inducing comments about mommy sleeping with her eyes open and not waking up. The kids got dressed, ate, and were out the door to school thanks to the gracious angels who were driving them. I was quickly on the road back to the hospital—with fountains, of course.

When I got there, Melanie had little pads glued to her head, and she didn't look very happy.

"I meeean…" She pointed at her head as soon as she saw me.

"It's a nice look," I told her.

The nurse came in the room right after me.

"Can you call down and find out when this guy is coming back?" Melanie asked the nurse immediately.

"He hasn't been back yet?" the nurse asked.

"No!" Melanie exclaimed. "And it's been like two hours!"

"I'll call down there when I get done here," the nurse said.

I was trying to walk around the bed, but a big contraption was in my way. "What's this?" I asked.

"That's the guy's equipment!" Melanie said.

"He just left it here for two hours?" I asked.

"Yeah!"

"You think he'd need that, wherever he is," I said, staring at the big machine on wheels.

"Just push it out of your way."

"I don't want to break it," I said. "This thing probably costs more than our house."

So, we sat there with a portable EEG machine at the end of the bed and Melanie's head covered with little irritating pads. Melanie interrogated the nurse while she was in there and then went back to working Sylvia. Doctors and nurses and technicians kept parading through, and we kept asking all of them if they could get the EEG guy back up here or else get these pads off her.

"I'm pulling these things off," Melanie said during a pause in the parade a few hours later.

"Don't!" I insisted. "You're on blood thinners and those are glued on. If you rip a bunch of skin off and start bleeding, you might not be able to stop bleeding."

She rolled her eyes and sighed.

"Well, can you go find someone to get these off?"

"Who am I going to ask? We've already asked everyone in the hospital." I paused. "Well, except for the EEG guy because he's the only one that no one can find."

Finally, in the early afternoon, the team of doctors I'd been hearing about came in. So many doctors and specialists were evaluating and treating Melanie that I had no idea who they all were. The head of this team wasn't Melanie's oncologist, who had become Melanie's primary care provider. The head doctor, whatever her title was, was the primary care provider for Melanie's current stay in the hospital and the immediate treatment she was getting for the stroke and its aftermath. She was in charge of this unit of the hospital. We briefly met the head doctor yesterday but without the rest of the team.

This doctor was clearly an authority figure. Everything about her—her demeanor, mannerisms, and her way of speaking—presented as a professional accustomed to making decisions and having people follow her orders. She was impressive. Her entourage of several other doctors gathered around her like minions, and they obviously deferred to her. This was the second time the full team had been in to see Melanie, but they had come early in the morning the day before when I was getting kids off to school and driving to the hospital.

Melanie forewarned me about Number Two. She couldn't stand him. He was apparently being groomed for a larger future role, and the head doctor generally stayed back and had him do most of the talking. They asked who I was and went through introductions and formalities, and then it was time to get to the medical discussion. The head doctor nodded to one of her minions, who I suspected was Number Two, although I wasn't certain yet.

As soon as he started talking, Melanie bellowed a long, drawn-out, "Noooooo!"

I mentioned before that Melanie could be a little hardheaded and stubborn. As much as Melanie loved people overall, she was like me in that she mostly divided people up into two categories: those who are not assholes and those who are assholes. Melanie could bond with someone almost instantly, but she didn't tolerate the assholes. I found her judgment of people to be so flawless that I typically went with her conclusions.

Although I'd suspected which one was Number Two, the bellowed "Noooooo!" confirmed it. He had physically separated himself from the group. The rest of them were at the side of the bed and grouped back toward the door, but he was the lone person standing at the end of the bed.

Despite my gut feeling to agree with Melanie, I gestured to her and gave her a look to give Number Two a chance. This was too important. This wasn't a case of not liking someone you meet at a friend's party or at a church function. We were in a life-and-death battle with cancer and strokes and who knows what else lurking in her systems. If the medical team felt it was best to proceed this way, then I wanted to hear them out that way.

The moment he started talking, I understood why Melanie didn't like him. He was cocky and condescending. Every word out of his mouth made me want to punch him in the mouth. Despite that, I listened to what he had to say, and I even asked him a clarifying question or two.

"We will be discharging her this afternoon," he said after he had explained a little more.

"NOOOOO!" This time, the word boomed out of my mouth. "Absolutely not!"

I was done with Number Two. Melanie was right, as usual, and I had no use for that guy anymore. I turned to the head doctor. Number Two started to say something. I raised my hand and waved him off, and I saw the minions' eyes widen and jaws drop when I did.

■ ■ ■ ■ ■ ■

I consider myself an exceptionally reasonable person. I believe in brains over brawn and prefer to negotiate rather than fight. I'm not afraid of confrontation. I avoid it logically—not out of fear, although there is always a degree of fear in anyone, whether they admit it or not. When I was younger, I was meek and afraid of everything, but I've already told you that backstory.

The first time I realized I had come full circle, from frightened little boy to a confident man, was with Melanie. We had been planning our wedding for months, and then one day, Melanie told me her dad, Daun, wanted to meet with us. He didn't tell her why. She speculated that Daun might be offering to help pay for some of it, something he had not done up until that time. However, Melanie also warned me how unpredictable her dad was and that this could be about almost anything. I already knew plenty about their story, including that he was an alcoholic and somewhat abusive.

Although I'd heard numerous stories about him, I had only met him a couple times. From those meetings, Melanie's stories seemed believable. While he had not displayed any abusive behavior in my presence, he was certainly obnoxious, including saying some oddly inappropriate things to his own daughters.

For this mystery meeting, we sat in his living room. Melanie and I sat on a couch near the front door with a coffee table in front of us. Across from us, Daun sat in a big cushioned chair.

"You kids are acting like a couple of idiots," he started the conversation. I felt Melanie squirm. This was exactly what she had been dreading. It was unlikely that he would offer to pay for the wedding. "First of all, you haven't even been together long enough to get married."

"Why not?" I calmly asked him.

"Because," he looked incredulous, "you barely know each other. You can't go jumping into something like this."

"Who's jumping in?" Melanie yelled.

Daun shook his head, clearly confounded that we couldn't comprehend his wisdom.

"How long have we been together?" I asked him.

He stared back at me cluelessly. I waited for an answer.

"Well…" he finally said after a long pause.

"We were together for over nine months before we got engaged, which is longer than you knew your second wife before you married her, right?" I educated him. "Now, for some people that might be fast, but for others, that isn't fast at all. For the next four months, we barely did any wedding planning. Now we have a date set, and by the time we get married, we will have been together for nearly two and a half years."

I paused to see what he might say to that. He again shook his head, still clearly confounded.

Sometimes I can be a bit of a smart-ass myself, and he had put me in a mood.

"Maybe you can show me your book," I suggested.

"What book?" He seemed confused by that.

"Well, clearly you must have a book that says exactly how long people should date before they get engaged and then how long they should be engaged before they get married. I'm just wondering what your book says."

"HA!" Melanie cackled. She did that a lot. When something really struck her, she would let out one loud exploding "HA!" I would hear that thousands of times over the years.

Daun didn't find my sarcasm quite as amusing.

"You're not seeking wise counsel!" he bellowed.

Now it was mine turn to stare at him incredulously. I meeean…, *who talks like that?*

"*Wise counsel?*" I sort of thought out loud. The words hung in the air for a couple seconds. "What wise counsel?"

"Me!" he bellowed again. "You need to respect your elders." He was up on his feet, quite agitated, which fell perfectly in line with the stories Melanie had told me about him. "You need to be coming to me for advice. I've been there, and you dumbass kids don't have a clue what you're doing or what you're getting into!"

This was so ridiculous that it could be considered amusing, but I was starting to get a little agitated myself.

"So…what…you want to help pick out the cake?" I asked.

"HA!" Melanie cackled again, but I noted a tone of nervousness in it now. Daun's face was getting red.

"This is serious!" he screamed.

"Okay, dad," Melanie said, and I could definitely hear the tension in her voice. "Let's just calm down."

Although there was a coffee table between him and us, he lunged toward Melanie, sticking his finger in her face. "You better listen…" He started to scream with an unacceptable level of intensity, but it was his threatening physical posture that brought me to my feet. Actually, that was only one part of it.

I'm a big guy, and I was always an athlete. Despite struggling with confidence due to my childhood issues, I still participated in sports throughout most of my life. I wrestled in high school, and despite a lack of wins or success, I made gains and improved by participating. In fact, those years in wrestling were a huge part of the foundation of my character that enabled me to begin turning my life around that day in my crappy apartment in Columbia. Whether a champion or the worst guy on the team, I've learned it is better to be in the ranks learning and developing than to be wasting idly away. Every effort is beneficial and pays dividends in some way.

While working my way through college, one of my jobs was working as a bouncer in bars. I was accustomed to jumping into the middle of fights, pulling bodies out of the fray, and dragging irate gents out of the building. At the time of this encounter with Melanie's dad, I stood 6'5", weighed over 240 pounds, could bench press over 400 pounds, and knew how to handle myself—and others. I don't mean to be the kind of meathead guy who talks about how much he can bench press, since that means little in life, but I'm trying to paint a picture here. If skinny old Daun thought he was going to intimidate me, he didn't know what he was getting into. When Daun took a physically threatening posture toward Melanie, it was time to educate him on some new realities.

"SIT DOWN AND SHUT UP!" My voice boomed through the house, reverberating off the walls. I was up and looming over him, face-to-face.

His eyes filled with shock and fear, and he immediately stepped back. He raised his arms, palms out, in a capitulating gesture as he fell back into the chair. I have to admit, I was kind of disappointed. I do believe in discretion and reason over violence, but I'm also human, and I was a young guy at the time. Only a few years earlier, Daun might have been one of those neighborhood dads that I would have been terrified to encounter, and I would have cowered in his presence.

Now, I wanted the fight for a whole slew of reasons, not the least of which was protecting Melanie. I was madly in love with her and having the time of my life with her, and I wanted a degree of payback for the stories I had heard about how he'd treated her over the years.

No one, not Daun or anyone else, was going to treat her like that ever again. I felt the confidence and power I had developed over the past several years, and I was resolute in that it was time to establish some boundaries in our relationship with Daun. I intended to send clear notice to him that he would never be treating her, or us, this way again. Now—exemplifying the textbook bully that he was—he was the one cowering like a coward.

"We'll do whatever we want to do, and you won't say a thing about it!" My voice continued to roar. "If you want to write us a check and pay for at least part of this wedding, maybe you can say something about it. Otherwise, just shut your damn mouth! And that goes for every other aspect of our life and every decision we *ever* make."

Daun looked terrified, and I was fine with that. I was ready to pound him right through the floor, and he could see it. After only meeting me a couple times before, I think he had misjudged me. I'm not much on bravado, typically. My usual demeanor is laid-back, and I'm more likely to behave like a goofy kid than an alpha male. To me, bravado typically comes off looking like stupidity. I believe this caused Daun to misjudge me and underestimate me, which I think happens with me a lot in life, but I don't really care if most people underestimate me because there is rarely a need to call out the beast that dwells within. That beast is better left caged, and he isn't any fun anyway. I prefer fun, which was probably one of the main reasons I ended up with Melanie. Daun had brought out the beast, and he would never underestimate me again.

Daun still had his hands raised, palms out, waving them in surrender.

"No, no." He was shaking his head. "You misunderstood me."

Pathetic.

This crude, crusty old man, who would have intimidated me in my younger years, looked and sounded like the pathetic coward he was. He epitomized the narcissistic bully. Apparently, I had misunderstood all his rantings. There was no apology. No acknowledgment that he had overstepped his bounds, or anything else of the kind. This entire thing was just a big misunderstanding due to my inability to decipher what a great guy he was from his little tirade. I sat back down as he rambled on with his explanations of our misunderstandings and our misinterpretations of his benevolence and magnanimity. I felt like The Godfather. I just sat back, allowing him to ramble for a minute or two.

"Anything else?" I said to him and then looked at Melanie. She looked empowered, like she was suppressing elation. She gave me a slight smile and said, "Let's go." She said a little more to her dad and gave him a hug. I shook his hand, and he tried to say something clever.

The father of the bride never offered to contribute a dollar for his daughter's wedding, but I have to give credit where credit is due. After the wedding, he gave us a check for a couple thousand dollars. It was only a small fraction of what it had cost, but it was something. What we would discover years later is that he was really giving Melanie back a small fraction of the wealth of inheritance he had stolen from her, but that's a story I won't even get into.

When we got into the car, Melanie threw her arms around me. "No one has ever stood up for me like that before." Although tears clouded her eyes, she seemed elated and giddy, and she started kissing me all over my face. "I can't believe you talked to him like that!" she exclaimed.

Melanie had other family who certainly would have put Daun in his place and stood up for her, but they all lived in another state hundreds of miles away. While they knew Daun wasn't exactly a father-of-the-year candidate, they didn't have the exposure or opportunity to do anything about it. Melanie wasn't helpless either. She handled Daun well on her own overall, but relationships can be complicated, and without allies, a misguided authority figure can certainly cause perpetual distress, and the parent-child relationship is especially unique.

Despite my description of him and our rough start, I got along with Daun over the years. He was the bad-boy teenager who never grew up, with an impish charm that could draw people to him. He loved deeply. Melanie and I recognized that his vices and his temper demanded caution when interacting with him. We enjoyed our time with him, but we remained vigilant to maintain a safe buffer in our affairs with him.

Daun would never be anything but nice to me, and his relationship with Melanie was forever changed. He would treat her respectfully whenever I was around. He would be somewhat worse when I wasn't around. She would notice this and even joke about it with me. If she went to visit him without me, he would act like a jerk, but nothing like the way he used to treat her. When I thought about our visit with Daun, I realized that Melanie had never seen that side of me before either. And for the next two decades, she wouldn't see the beast again. But whether it was Daun or anyone else in our world, there was never a need to unleash the beast, at least not until cocky and condescending Number Two told us they were going to discharge her that afternoon.

■ ■ ■ ■ ■ ■

I had raised my hand to Number Two and waved him off as I turned to the head doctor. I stole a glance at Melanie as I shifted in the chair and squared my shoulders to the doctor. Melanie looked scared. She did not want to go home. She didn't want to be having strokes or unexplained episodes in front of the kids, and she didn't want to go home again just to be calling 9-1-1 minutes later as we had done before. I wasn't assuming any of this. I knew all this because we had already talked about it, and I was in total agreement. It wasn't only me protecting her; it was us mutually protecting our kids.

"I'm not taking her home just to have another stroke and have to call 9-1-1 and be right back in here." I looked the head doctor straight in the eye and spoke forcefully. "We have four little kids at home, and she keeps having strokes or episodes that no one seems to be able to explain to us. I'm not taking her home just to terrify the kids by making them watch her have another stroke or another one of these episodes—whatever they are."

The beast remained caged on this one. It had popped its head out and let out a roar, but I contained it. I was speaking to the head doctor respectfully yet firmly. I did feel a little like The Godfather again. The head doctor may have been the authority to everyone else around, but no one else was making this call. I didn't care what the head doctor or any doctors or hospital administrators or the insurance company wanted to do. Melanie was not being discharged. Period. End of discussion. If they insisted on discharging her, the cage was bursting open.

I watched the head doctor's face closely. She was impressive. She kept her composure perfectly, and I could tell she was seriously considering my words. The minions looked professionally stunned. They were mostly staying composed, but I could tell they were shocked by the way I was talking to the head doctor, and probably also by the way I'd dismissed Number Two. A couple of them turned and looked inquisitively at the head doctor, who seemed to be cogitating on my statements.

"What are these episodes she keeps having?" I asked after a long pause. I stated it less like a question and more like a challenge to them to answer it. "When are these going to end, if ever? Do you even know what they are? If you don't, just tell us that. If you do, why the hell can't anyone explain it to us? At least we'll understand something about what we're dealing with. Is there anything you can do about all this? What does life look like once we get home? I don't know what we're going to do for her or how we're going to handle this when we get home, and I don't have any reason to believe that we won't be headed right back to the hospital within hours, and I'm not—*we* are not—putting our kids through that. You do know that we have four little kids at home, don't you?"

The head doctor nodded at that last statement. "I do know you have kids," she said calmly before taking the time to collect her thoughts. "And I do understand your concerns. You raise some very good points." I was getting a feeling of mutual respect between us. This was drastically different than the discussion with Daun, and I appreciated how she handled this. "Let us do this…" She paused again to arrange her thoughts. "Our team will review Melanie's information and confer, and we will address your concerns before we make any decisions."

"Thank you!" I said in a respectful tone. "We appreciate that."

I saw the relief and gratitude on Melanie's face. I had her back, and she appreciated it. She nodded and smiled slightly as she looked me in the eye.

"And could you please, *please*, get someone in here to take these damn pads off her head?"

The head doctor looked confused by that request.

"The EEG tech, or whoever it was, came in here *hours* ago and put them on her," I explained, "and then left without running any tests and has not come back. I meeeean...did he get mad and quit? Where'd he go? Is he coming back? Can someone else just take these off her if he isn't coming back?"

"Uh, we'll make a call down and see what we can find out about that," the head doctor said. A few more statements were made, and then the doc and her minions left the room.

I'm sure those doctors are accustomed to patients and their families and friends yelling and screaming and otherwise questioning them all the time, and it probably does not change the patient's situation much. But whatever they thought of what I had said to them, Melanie did not get discharged that day. We didn't hear back from any of those doctors the rest of the day, but the nurse came in a couple hours later and informed us that Melanie was not being discharged. She would be staying at least another night in this room.

Melanie slept for a while, and then they took her out for some more tests. While she was gone, Sylvia was discharged. As she was leaving, Sylvia handed me a piece of paper with her phone number on it. She was gushing about how much she adored Melanie and asked if we would please give her a call and let her know how Melanie was doing. Once again, I was amazed how quickly and easily Melanie could bond with someone in any circumstance. In all the shuffling of hospital paperwork and all the other activity, I would somehow lose Sylvia's paper, and I felt bad about that. I'm sure Melanie would have wanted to call her later.

I went back to answering the ongoing stream of text messages, and then I fell asleep in the chair until Melanie was brought back in. Our friend Tiffani showed up right after that and had brought Melanie a fountain.

"Oh, sorry, Paddy, I should have gotten you one too," Tiffani said.

The nurse came in to do something to Melanie, and Tiffani and I stepped into the hallway for a moment.

"Her speech has gotten worse," I informed Tiffani. "Each time she has one of those episodes, it goes away again and then comes back again, but each time it doesn't come back as well. She's struggling a lot more, and it's harder to figure out what she's trying to say."

Tiffani had been in to see Melanie multiple times and had been the one who took Melanie into the hospital when she had the first stroke, the Vision Stroke, and had stayed much of that weekend with her while I was taking care of the kids. Tiffani was already familiar with the episodes and most of everything else that had been going on. She thought for a bit about what I had told her and nodded.

"That's okay, Paddy. I, too, speak Melanie in all its forms," Tiffani said. Tiffani was one of Melanie's closest friends, part of the inner circle, and she could practically read Melanie's mind and finish her sentences about as well as I could, sometimes even better, depending on the topic of discussion.

"You should get something to eat," Melanie said when we got back into the room. "When is the last time you ate?"

It was currently about five in the evening. "Uh, I ate at the house this morning," I lied. I think I had eaten something sometime the day before, but I couldn't remember it. I rushed out of the house this morning, and I knew I had not eaten even as I got the kids breakfast and their lunches ready. Oddly, I didn't feel hungry, but they were probably right that I should eat. While I knew Melanie was concerned about me, sending me off to eat was probably also code for wanting to have girl talk with Tiffani and get me out of the way.

For maybe the first time in my life, food wasn't appealing. I went into the hospital cafeteria and looked over the menus. They had a few sections of different types of food, but nothing sounded good. I finally went with old faithful and got a burger and fries from the grill. I ate some of it and headed back up to the room.

When I got back, the pads were finally gone from Melanie's head—over 10 hours after they had been put on for tests that were never done.

"Oh, did the EEG guy *finally* come back?" I asked. Melanie looked a little squeamish about that one, which told me all I needed to know. She knew I'd be mad if she pulled them off herself.

"The nurse helped her do it," Tiffani said.

"Uh-huh." I looked skeptically at her. That sounded like a well-conceived cover story.

"No, she really did," Tiffani elaborated. Being a lawyer, she was accustomed to pleading a case. "They tried one and it came off easily enough, so then they took off the rest."

It still might have been a cover story. This might have been part of the motivation for sending me off to dinner. I let it go. It didn't matter; it was done. Melanie was more comfortable, and she wasn't bleeding profusely from her head. And since an entire hospital full of medical professionals couldn't get this done all day, I couldn't really blame her for taking matters into her own hands. I was actually surprised those things stayed on her head that long.

The three of us hung out for at least a couple hours, although Melanie dozed off a few times. Other visitors came, and Tiffani was still there, so I headed home to be with the kids. I didn't sleep much again that night, but Melanie's mystery episodes were happening less frequently and less intensely. With my thoughts somewhat less frantic and erratic, I might have gotten a few hours of sleep off and on.

The morning went much like the previous one, and I was back at the hospital, with his-and-her fountains, by midmorning.

"Hey!" I said as I walked in the room. She was smiling.

"I did not..." She was struggling with her words, which had become more apparent and possibly more permanent. "...have..." She gulped on the next word, "eh..."

"You didn't have an episode?" I filled in.

She nodded, smiling. "All night!" The words were gargled but clear enough for me.

"*Suck it, Trebek!*" I exclaimed, and we high-fived.

"So, you haven't had one since yesterday afternoon?" I asked, and she responded by nodding.

The nurse came in and we all talked for a bit. The nurse seemed positive about Melanie's condition and her improvement. Melanie wanted to get up and move, which was a good sign. It was especially important considering she recently had at least one blood clot in her leg on top of the stroke-inducing clots. The hallways in this area formed an H. Her room was near the middle of one of the legs of the H. We walked to the end of the hallway and back up, which was probably less than 100 feet in total but took us a while as she could barely shuffle along. She was clinging to my arm with one hand and leaning onto her cane with the other. We came back up the hall and turned into the connecting hallway to the other leg of the H. We came to the front of the nurses' station, and another nurse came down the hallway toward us.

"Hey, look at you, Melanie!" the nurse walking to us said.

"Great to see you up!" one of the nurses sitting in the station said. "Good for you!"

Melanie made jokes about how she was moving, and before I knew it, three or four nurses gathered around us. Another patient was down the hallway and joined our impromptu hallway group party, calling Melanie by name. I wondered how they would all know her name, particularly the other patient, who I had never seen before. I was with Melanie most of the day, and she hadn't been walking around much. Maybe she did at night? Even though I wondered how they would all know her and seem so delighted to see her, it didn't surprise me. That was Melanie. As they all chattered away, I thought back to when Melanie started chemo.

■ ■ ■ ■ ■

I took Melanie to her first chemo infusion. The treatment room was a large open room with recliners circled around. When we entered, the room was nearly full yet very quiet. The mood was dismal, and everyone looked gloomy, which is almost an understatement. I'm sure chemo is different for everyone. There are multiple chemo drugs and dosages, along with other considerations. Melanie was on an aggressive regiment administering three different chemo drugs, so her infusions took hours. After infusions, there would be this odd delay of a couple days, and then she would get extremely sick and be absolutely miserable. She would lay in bed moaning and crying in pain. After the first treatment, she found a friend who let her stay over at her house during those days so our kids wouldn't hear all that and get scared. If any of the patients in this room experienced even a fraction of the side effects that Melanie suffered, it was easy to understand why they would all appear so despondent, without even considering all the other emotional anxieties of being a cancer patient. I specifically recall one lady who appeared to be in her sixties, although she might have been younger. I've seen firsthand how the effects of cancer can quickly add years to a patient's appearance. This woman looked utterly dejected. She wore a pink and purple wrap on her head with some sort of large pin in it. She sat slumped over in her chair with her chin dropped onto her chest. She barely moved, although I could tell she was awake.

Melanie was immediately cracking jokes and making conversation with her nurse, and then she got other patients talking and laughing along. The entire mood of the room notably improved within minutes, and soon laughter was prevalent. Once again, Melanie raised the spirits of everyone around her, but this was a new level even for her, taking an ordinary and unpleasant event and transforming it into something extraordinary. A room that had felt morbid and macabre was now infused with laughter and friendly conversation. At one point, I even saw the pink-and-purple headwrap lady smile.

I hadn't seen anything yet.

Melanie received chemo infusions every three weeks. I couldn't take her for the second infusion, so our friend Vivian, another in the inner circle, took her. I wanted to be there for her, especially now that I'd seen the aftereffects and knew how much she was dreading that. I took an early lunch and headed to the hospital. When I entered, I wound through the maze of hallways toward the treatment room in the back of the building. From the front of the building, I could hear laughter and shouting in the distance, and I assumed there was a staff birthday party or something like that going on. The closer I got to the treatment room, the louder it got, and it sounded like a lively party. I thought it odd that the staff would throw such a raucous party in a building full of patients needing rest for recovery.

I should have known better.

I turned the final corner in the hallway to the large swinging doors into the treatment room, and the noise could have knocked me over. Melanie's closest friends were a group that could not only keep up with her, but also shared much of her spirit and mastery of good times. Vivian had brought games, mostly trivia questions on little cards. Melanie and Vivian were like cohosts of some wild rumpus, and it felt like I'd walked into a birthday party for a bunch of screeching nine-year-old kids. Bald-headed adult cancer patients with tubes and wires sticking out of their bodies screamed answers while cackling and laughing hysterically, as if they had just won the lottery. I leaned against the wall and stood there watching for a few minutes, utterly amazed by the joy and laughter. I heard someone scream out, "I know that one!" I looked over, and the pink-and-purple headwrap lady was bouncing on the edge of her seat, raising her hand like an excited fourth-grader eager to be called on and thrilled when she got to shout out the answer. The more life tried to knock Melanie down, the higher she rose above it—and she lifted others up with her.

■ ■ ■ ■ ■ ■

So that day in the hospital, as we walked the H and a quiet little impromptu party formed around Melanie in front of the nurses' station, it seemed normal. This was our ordinary. The group disbanded after a few minutes of jokes and laughter. Melanie and I continued walking the H, and she fielded more banter passing the nurses' station on the second lap.

When we got to the end of the hallway, it was a process simply to turn around. She painstakingly shifted her feet in numerous little steps as she pivoted around her cane, then let out a deep breath from the exertion. My once-vibrant 45-year-old wife was hunched over and moving like she was 90.

"You wouldn't sign up for this again," she said in fragmented speech. She made a poor attempt to make it sound like a joke, but a clear tone of truthful anxiety laced that comment.

I rolled my eyes and shook my head. This was something she had said to me multiple times before, especially over the last few months, which was the same timespan since the diagnosis of the tumor in her liver. I took offense to this comment, as I had every other time. I am a loyal person. I felt that she should have understood and respected my loyalty, especially after all we'd been through. Of course, I understood that she was dealing with an overload of fears and emotions that was causing her to reflect on every aspect of her life, but I was irked that she questioned my loyalty and doubted my commitment and love for her, especially having done so repeatedly over a significant span of time. It wasn't an isolated comment or feeling.

I realized later that I shouldn't have been annoyed with her. No relationship is perfect. I've been annoyed by and fought with every friend I've ever had—and they have been annoyed with me as well. As a kid, I'd get enraged with my parents. As a parent, I've gotten frustrated with my kids. If I ever meet a married couple that didn't fight and annoy each other in numerous ways, I'd be stunned. Actually, I wouldn't be stunned. I'd know it was a lie—total bullshit.

Melanie and I endured innumerable moments of anger, doubt, and annoyance with one another. That's life. It doesn't mean I didn't love her. After an argument, I had had another significant revelation—The Escape Clause Revelation—that elevated my comprehension of our relationship, and all relationships, to an entirely new level.

6

The Cowbell Guy

About a year and a half earlier, Melanie and I had an epic fight. In many ways, it was similar to numerous other fights we had over the years, but this fight defined our relationship like no other. Reflecting later on things that felt so serious, so grave, so dire, or otherwise important at the time, I realized how silly and inconsequential most of these things actually were. I'm grateful I learned these lessons early enough.

This epic fight redefined our understanding of our greatest conflict. This was the final major clash of my ambition versus her risk aversion. It was my desire to achieve and improve our financial situation through professional accomplishment versus her focus on family and relationships. As is often the case with marital conflicts, it started over something that, in retrospect, would seem quite trivial.

"Okay, everybody!" she yelled across the house. "It's family cleanup time!"

F***ing family cleanup time. That pretty much sums up how I felt about that.

I'd been working on a software system that I believed could be highly profitable and therefore change our entire financial situation. This was a few years after my company had been shut down, and Melanie had no interest in going through anything like that again.

In my spare time, mostly at night after the kids were put to bed and Melanie took her slew of nighttime drugs and went catatonic, I would get back to coding until I couldn't keep my eyes open any longer.

I was dealing with an infuriating error, an agonizing bug in the code that was preventing other development and stalling my progress for days. I was in no mood for distractions, diversions, or interruptions. I was primed to erupt. In addition to my usual ambition, I was working with an amplified sense of urgency to provide for our future, considering Melanie's condition. While her health seemed stable, it had a reached a stage where it lingered as a continuous concern, a nagging inevitability, even if still a distant eventuality.

Melanie had mostly recovered from her first spinal fusion surgery. She was walking slowly but decently without a cane or other implement. The other fractures in her vertebrae that would more restrictively limit her mobility were still unknowingly in our future. She had not yet been diagnosed with the liver tumor, and radiation was well in the past. She was on chemo pills and was tested monthly to monitor the state of her cancer. Even then, we were watching her numbers continuously. She was only on about 17 medications at this point, so nothing was too terribly desperate in our relative world of cancer. The fears and the realities remained mostly submerged, but a few fins were starting to stick up out of the water, reminding us what lurked beneath the surface. We feared those predators would surface sooner or later.

Melanie was visibly deteriorating, although I believed most of it was temporary. I remained doggedly positive that she would recover from each setback, but then there always seemed to be another setback. Since she had been diagnosed with Wegener's the year before the cancer diagnosis, it had been three years of one setback after another. Her diminished capacity to work and supplement our income was further decreasing by the month, and there were no signs of her returning to a regular job any time soon, if ever. While I strove to remain positive, especially around her and the kids, there was a lurking fear of the future, and with that fear came a determination to get us in a better position to handle any of cancer's consequences. I wasn't delusional or in denial, but sometimes you have to consider the imminence of that which doesn't seem imminent and set your priorities accordingly. I was in the middle of things that I didn't understand, and that demanded the constant reevaluation of priorities.

Family cleanup time was not my priority.

I'd appease her. I got up and grabbed a few loose toys off the floor and tossed them on a shelf. The kids could do the rest. I wondered why I was even involved. Nearly everything to be cleaned up was kids' toys and clothes and such. Let the kids be responsible and clean up their own mess. I'd had enough of family cleanup time. I was back on my computer on the soft side of 30 seconds.

She and the kids finished up in about ten minutes, which only confirmed to me that I didn't need to be involved, and then we started the bedtime routine. I gave the youngest two baths, brushed their teeth, helped them get into pajamas, put them in bed, and sang the songs they always insisted upon. I enjoyed this. Fortunately, they were too young to realize how terrible my singing is. Even though this was time I typically enjoyed with the kids, my mind was preoccupied, slogging through a swamp of cryptically coded and maddeningly obscured errors.

Melanie put the older two to bed, which was less involved since they mostly took care of themselves. She then began piling random stuff on the table right next to me, strategically placing items to crowd my space, as if she were still worried about cleaning the house. It was childish and immature to me, so it was a perfect exemplification of marital discord. The swelling pile was all stuff of mine. There were a couple of books, some papers, keys, and whatever else.

I swept my arm across the table and swept the entire pile right onto the floor—but in a totally reserved and mature way.

"Well, that was mature," she snarled. But see, she agreed.

"Whatever," I cleverly rebuked.

"And *thanks* for all your support!" she chided.

"The kids cleaned up just fine." I looked around the room, which was tidy and clean now. "It didn't even take them that long. They didn't need my help."

"That's *not* the point!" She seemed unusually upset over this one, and her elevated anger made me more agitated. "We've talked about this…*so many times*! You said you would support me on this!" Family cleanup time was a serious endeavor to Melanie. It wasn't just about the cleaning. It was much more about the routines and lessons we were teaching the children, and we *had* discussed it many times.

She was right about all of that, and yet I just didn't care. The very word "support" had become almost taboo in our world, as neither of us ever felt supported by the other. Even though she was right, I wasn't about to concede anything, especially when the S-word was involved. Maturity was oozing out of me from every pore.

"Like you—" I started to say it, but I stopped myself. First, I had to redirect the conversation because I was losing—badly. She was right about everything she was saying. I knew it, but I was in no mood to admit it. My only option was to redirect like a dipshit politician. My instincts were to slam on the brakes, but it was already far too late to stop this train.

"What?" Melanie exclaimed.

It was definitely too late. She wasn't letting that one go.

"Were you going to say that *I* don't *support* you? Oh, *please* don't tell me you were going to say *that*!"

I was losing on every point in this argument, and my redirect had backfired. It wasn't looking too good for me. The unresolvable issue of support was a vexing point of contention that had been lingering in our realm for many years. I wished I hadn't said what I'd said, not because it upset her, but because it pissed me off. Worse, I didn't have an answer as to why. I couldn't go down this road, even though I believed I was right, because I couldn't define what I felt. It was odd, and it had always felt odd to me.

I had not felt supported by Melanie for years, and I'd commented on that numerous times, yet I couldn't explain why. She had asked me many times what it would take for me to feel supported by her, and for some reason, I could never find the answer. I didn't feel I was wrong, but my frustration on the topic was amplified by my own inability to identify it or define it, which frustrated her even more than it frustrated me.

"How many times have I asked you to tell me what me supporting you would look like to you?" she asked.

I let out a sigh, annoyed by her truth and frustrated by my inability to counter it.

"Can you tell me *anything* I could do that would make you feel supported?"

My annoyance morphed into aggravation.

"I've given you time to go work or write so many times over the years."

This was true, but it only amplified my aggravation. While she was right, something about it only incensed me.

"How many times do you think I've stayed home alone or taken care of the kids while you went off to work on…whatever it was at the time?"

Again, she was right, but it only escalated my anger ever higher.

"I've agreed to invest our savings—and every other dollar we had!"

So true, and now my rage was on the cusp of the boiling point.

"So, what does it look like? Tell me how I can make you feel supported! I've been asking you to explain this to me for years, and you *still* can't do it!"

"I want you to *believe* in me!" I screamed. I don't know where it came from, but I instantly felt the truth in it.

She had no response. She stood motionless and stared blankly at me. The words hung in the air. In her face, I saw the same shock that I was feeling. I'd said it, but I almost didn't realize what I'd said.

That was *IT*.

That was the answer to the question she'd been asking me for probably close to two decades. I never realized it before. I had never been able to identify it or define it, but that was it. My own statement stunned me, and it tore open the flood gates.

"I want you to get excited about something I'm doing—*anything* I'm doing—as if you actually believe I'll succeed."

"Well, what does that look like?" The question sounded as empty and desperate as the look on her face.

"I don't know. I mean…you never ask anything about my system. You never ask how it's going. You never ask to see it. If you believed in me and cared about any of it, you'd ask to see it or at least ask about how it's going from time you time. You'd even be excited by the possibilities and what it could mean for our future. You *never have!*"

Melanie was a talker. She was certainly a good listener too. For over 20 years, it seemed like the only time she ever stopped talking was when she was listening, but conversation never stopped. With Melanie, there's always something to discuss. There was always something else to say. I'd never, ever seen her speechless—until this moment. Her face was beyond blank; it was devoid of all expression.

"Do you even believe I'm going to succeed?" I asked.

She looked down at the floor without a word, and that told me everything.

I was gone.

I couldn't be there.

I walked past her and grabbed my keys and wallet. I walked past her again as I headed out of the room, and she just stood there silently, looking lost.

I got in the car with no idea where I was going. I drove a familiar route out of habit. After a bit, I turned onto Interstate 44, heading west away from the city. I cut through the remainder of the suburbs. The highway was crowded by buildings and structures for several miles, until the fourth lane pinched itself off and the highway narrowed, one more avenue lost in the journey. With each exit, the buildings and structures conceded as the empty countryside asserted its dominance. It could have been a beautifully scenic drive, but the light abandoned me as the sun fell. Leafless trees took the form of nefarious creatures with jagged arms poised to slice me to shreds if I deviated off my allotted path.

The third lane pinched itself off, narrowing my options again as another pathway deserted me. Off the highway, I caught a glimpse of a decrepit trailer court I had driven past many times. A sign out front declared it as Paradise, and who was I to say it wasn't. I continued into the void of the desolate and darkened countryside, seething the entire way.

The number one thing I wanted in my entire life was someone to believe in me. Doesn't everyone? In Melanie, I'd been living under the delusion that I had found that someone. She was the most caring, positive, compassionate, and supportive person I had ever met. She wasn't that way only with me—at least, as I'd apparently wrongly considered her to be toward me. She was that way toward nearly everyone she met. Yet, now I found myself cruising through the darkness of my disillusionment in an epiphany of deceit.

I felt betrayed. I felt like I'd been living a lie. Had I wrongly assumed she believed in me all these years? *How could this be my life?* How could I have misunderstood every moment of the past 20 years? I was livid. I was angry in a way I'd never felt before.

How was I such a fool not to see this years ago? It had been right in front of me throughout our relationship. I could see it now, and it made sense out of so much of our time together. That realization devastated me.

I kept driving. I had moved to Los Angeles when I graduated college. I stayed out there less than a year. I had driven out there, and this was the same route I had taken back then. Maybe I'd keep going tonight and leave this miserable lie of a life behind me. I thought about going to California, but that was just fantasy. Just considering it made me realize it was time to turn around. I'd been driving for well over an hour, and I wasn't going anywhere.

During the drive back, I thought about comments Melanie had made over the years. I thought about the attitude she exhibited about so many of my efforts and ambitions. I suddenly saw her so differently. For the first time in close to 18 years of marriage, I seriously considered separation as an option. It was the first time I'd ever earnestly considered divorce. I felt as if I couldn't continue with this sham. How could I share time and space with someone who didn't believe in me? This seemed the worst-case scenario, and yet, somehow, I was there.

I'd thought about divorce before, of course. I wouldn't believe any married person who claimed they hadn't. At times, it was more of a musing. I would think of it as a what-if, like wondering what if I'd chosen a different career or played a sport or some other speculative daydream that lacked any substantial intention.

This was different. This felt real.

My feelings that I didn't want to be with her anymore felt deeply legitimate. I couldn't see how I could continue this life with her. I thought about how I might proceed. Would the cost and hassle of the process be worth the freedom and the opportunities that freedom would provide? What if I were unencumbered by the person I suddenly felt had been holding me back all these years? If I listed the top things I wanted in my marriage and from my partner, having someone who believed in me and was excited for what I could do would be the first thing on the list. And yet, I didn't have it. How could I not have seen this all these years? This situation now seemed intolerable, and divorce presented as a genuine option.

As I considered how divorce might play out, I immediately realized some weighty downsides. I would likely be shunned by our entire community and all our friends. I would look like the biggest asshole of the decade, maybe the century. Melanie was beloved in our community and beyond, and I'd be the asshole who left her while she was battling cancer with four little kids to take care of. I wouldn't be leaving the kids. I'd want joint custody, and I'd want to be in their lives. Our kids were awesome, and I love them infinitely, but then, what if our divorce caused bitterness in them and harmed my relationship with them? That deterrent terrified me, but I felt as if I couldn't handle living with her anymore. Although she was beloved in the community, those people didn't see below the surface. I'd be losing an entire community of loving and supportive friends and acquaintances, and maybe much more than that. It would be like getting released from one jail only to get thrown into another prison.

These reasons were compelling deterrents, and I was seriously considering them all on the drive home. Despite the substantial downsides, I was still considering if divorce was the best option. After all, while being shunned by your entire community was daunting and depressing, should I let the possible attitudes and judgments of others prevent me from doing what was best for me?

It was late when I got home. My round trip had taken well over three hours. The seething anger had mostly subsided, having deteriorated into bleak despair. Melanie had taken her batch of nighttime drugs and was deep asleep. I couldn't have woken her if I had wanted to, but I didn't want to. I sat on the edge of the bed and continued to stew about the sludge of discontentment my life had decomposed into.

Divorce, while momentarily appealing, seemed more and more inadvisable. On the other hand, continuing to live with this woman did not feel like an appealing option either. What else was there? The only other way out that I could even think of would be suicide, but that fleeting blip of a thought wasn't a consideration to me.

I still believed in me. I still believed in my abilities. I was still excited by the possibilities of what I could accomplish, even if I were the only one. While I realized that death would certainly get me out of this situation, it was a purely academic and transitory thought. I had no interest in that option. The entire idea of death seemed pointless, even though the thought of it had flickered briefly in my head.

And then it hit me. I suddenly realized I had an escape clause. Melanie had cancer. Melanie had a cancer so aggressive that it had metastasized even while she was doing chemo and radiation. She might live five or ten more years, and maybe they'd find a better treatment or cure during that time. But it was also possible that she might not make it more than another year or two, and a divorce would probably take that long anyway. Maybe it would keep being aggressive and keep spreading, and I'd be free. I'd be out of this and I wouldn't be the asshole.

I seriously considered this scenario. I started to imagine what it would be like to be free of these shackles of this marriage. What if I could come home like I did tonight and there would be no Melanie on the sofa? No Melanie in the kitchen or sitting at the table? I wouldn't have to answer to her or compromise with her. I would no longer have to deal with the constraints of her opinions or her wishes or her worries. I'd be independent and unencumbered. I sank into this scenario and projected myself into these visions of a future without her. What if I could sit here on the edge of this bed but there would be no Melanie next to me?

I'd be alone. I'd be without her. I'd put the kids to bed at night and sit in a quiet house—without my best friend.

These visions began to haunt me. I became terrified. I couldn't stop seeing the scenarios, and it felt horrifyingly real. It sickened me.

Throughout Melanie's cancer, I'd remained predominantly positive. From the beginning, I believed we would beat cancer. This was the first time I had acknowledged that Melanie may not be around forever. We might not grow old together and play with our grandkids together and travel the world in our golden years. She might be gone—sooner rather than later. I wasn't scared of being alone or lonely. I could handle that. I was terrified of not having Melanie. I was horror-struck by visions of a home, a life, and a world without her.

This was my Escape Clause Revelation. The revelation wasn't that I had this escape clause. The revelation was that I *didn't want* an escape clause. I wanted Melanie. I wanted her back to how she was before cancer. I wanted her around, even debilitated by this scourge. This was when I came to understand the depths of love. At times, it seems like love is deepest in the earliest stages, reaching its peak when we got engaged, married, and frolicked around as newlyweds. As the years went on, it morphed from love into partnership, at times feeling like we'd become partners running the joint businesses of household and family. We still cared deeply for one another and enjoyed our lives together, most of the time, but it could also feel like magic, excitement, and fun were displaced by commitment, responsibility, and obligation.

But I really felt the depths of my love for Melanie when the fear set in, when despair took hold, and when desperation and dread consumed me. With the strokes and the speech impairment and the tests and the days—weeks—in the hospital, my fears were amplified because I'd already faced them and understood them from The Escape Clause Revelation.

The Escape Clause Revelation revived my love and appreciation of Melanie, but it also birthed a conflict I couldn't tame. It was like a tornado attacking a tsunami—the interminable clash of unyielding forces. The conflict raged within me.

She was my best friend. She didn't believe in me.

She was the most extraordinary person I'd ever met. She couldn't get excited for me.

She was a rare and special gift. She saw my ambitions as a curse.

How could I live without her? How could I live with her?

For the next couple weeks, I brooded over these incongruous forces. We barely spoke, only enough to keep managing the household and caring for the kids. I realized more than ever how much I loved her and I wanted to live with her forever, but I didn't know how to cope with the disheartening realization that she didn't—and couldn't—support my ambitions and believe in me, at least not in the way I desired. It was dejecting.

But then, I also felt childish and weak. I felt that I should be tougher. At that point, I still didn't know what kind of tough I was supposed to be, but it was obvious I wasn't tough enough to stand on my own belief of myself. If I were, I wouldn't have these issues. Was I weak, or was I justified in my feelings? Once again, I was in the middle of something I didn't understand.

If I believed that Melanie should believe in me, then I was screwed because it was obvious that she wasn't capable. She wanted to be safe. She wanted her kids to live in a world of minimalized risk. She was never going to get excited about me introducing increased risk into our world. She didn't want me navigating anywhere off the safe and narrow path. Fortune may favor the bold, but contentment snuggles with the meek, and therein lurked the central conflict of our marriage.

As the next several days went by, I started feeling better about her and I began to form a new outlook on myself, but it was a mix of acceptance and animosity. I felt like I was forming the right conclusions. I developed a deeper comprehension of the reality of relationships. No one completes you—absolutely no one. This notion may sound good in fairy tales and romantic movies, but this falsehood is a danger to healthy relationships. Such fairy-tale ideals create unrealistic expectations and skewed perceptions that inevitably lead to disillusionment and disappointment.

I once read a book that explained that professional baseball scouts look for five key skills when evaluating players, and it's rare for any player to have all five. Many of the best professional athletes only possess three out of the five key skills to the degree that enables them to succeed at the highest levels. If a player has three out of five, he might become a legend and land in the hall of fame.

I concluded that marriage, or any relationship, is much the same. If I were to list what mattered to me and what I wanted and needed in our relationship, I might have come up with eight key things. Other people might come up with more or less, but everyone's list would be unique. But no matter how many or how few, the thing I realized is that no one gets them all. If you get five out of eight, you live a blessed and wonderful life—overall. No one lives happily ever after because that is a bullshit notion, in my humble opinion. I've learned that realistic expectations enable me to prepare for and cope with life's eventualities, while idealistic fairy-tale notions lead to devastation.

If I were to list my eight things, I think I had five or six of them in my relationship with Melanie, which was outstanding, even though one of the missing items was devastatingly the first one I would have listed—the single most important thing to me. If I had realized that years earlier, I might have made the worst decision of my life and not married Melanie. I was blessed by my own stupidity.

The Escape Clause Revelation launched a personal transformation exceeded only by my time at Parks College. I was again casting off part of who I was to grow into who I needed to be, but I had one serious impediment: I didn't know what that looked like or how to do it. I was one big walking mess of swirling thoughts and conflicting emotions.

After two weeks of brooding and contemplation, it was Melanie who broke down the wall, as it so often was. I was sitting on the edge of our bed putting on my shoes to go for a walk after the kids were in bed. She came in the room and stood at her dresser. I figured she was about to take her mound of nighttime drugs, but instead, she turned and faced me.

"Are you leaving us?"

The question caught me off guard. I heard the pain in her voice before seeing the fear in her eyes.

"No," I said definitively, without hesitation.

"So, what—are we just going to go on living together but not talking to each other?" she asked, with more frustration and less sarcasm than her usual. "The kids can see something is wrong. They've been asking me what's wrong with you lately." I didn't doubt that at all and instantly hated hearing it. I dreaded creating a negative environment for the kids, and that had to change.

"I love you," I said after taking a long pause to try to arrange my thoughts, which proved difficult. "You are the best friend I've ever had, and I love you now as much as I ever have, but..." I paused again, trying to figure out what I was even saying and how I wanted and needed to say it. "You aren't there for me. You don't—"

"Oh, and do you think you're there for *me*?" she cut me off.

"Don't turn this around and make this about you!" I shot back promptly. There was a history to this rebuke. Melanie had said those exact words to me countless times over the years in numerous arguments and discussions, and now I was throwing it back in her face—and it worked. She let it go; I almost did.

"I'm sure I'm not in some ways, but don't try to act like I'm not in *most* ways. I've stood by you..." I thought about the numerous points I could make on that, but that wasn't where we needed to go with this.

"Look," I paused, again figuring out how to say what I needed to say, "one of the biggest things I've realized in the past couple weeks is how much no relationship is perfect. I'm not perfect. You're not perfect. And together as a couple, we aren't perfect. This is why you have other friends. If we were perfect for each other and always there for each other, you wouldn't need other friends. Sometimes, I'm not the best person for you to talk to about things. Sometimes it's Stephanie. Sometimes it's Tiffani. Sometimes it's Vivian or Crutcher or Megan, or one of your other three thousand friends that you're always on the phone with. Different people fill different needs for each other, and that's okay. Right now, I'm trying to accept and figure out how to deal with the fact that you can't get excited about the things I'm working to accomplish. You don't believe in me in that way, and I have to deal with that, and that's okay, I guess. You're not wrong, and I'm not wrong. We're just different in this way, but right now I don't know how to feel about it or accept it or live with it, but I will. You're still the best friend I've ever had, and I still love you and want to be with you. I think we have it way better than most, but it isn't perfect—and sometimes, you're a pain in the ass."

Sometimes, communication really is amazing. It was shocking how saying all that out loud lifted the weight off instantly. As soon as I said these things to her, I felt better about everything, and I could tell she did too. It didn't erase all the pain, and I would continue to live with the disappointment, but it immediately felt manageable. We'd make it through this like we had made it through countless other struggles of all kinds. We sat on the bed and talked for at least another 30 minutes, and then she swallowed the mound of pills and went catatonic. I went for my walk.

As the days progressed, things were better than they had been in a long while. We weren't back to the crazy fun of the good old days, but we were enjoying our time together and having fun with the kids. Even with the lingering disappointment of newly discovered disenchantments, there was an enhanced comprehension of the depth of our relationship in the adjusted equilibrium of life and love.

A few weeks later, I was downstairs doing laundry late in the evening after the kids were in bed. I exited the laundry room and was jolted with surprise to see Melanie standing on the second step from the bottom of the stairs. It was especially unexpected because Melanie had not come down the stairs in months. With her spinal surgery and additional fractures, clunking down the stairs was too much for her.

"Did you move the Lego table?" she asked.

"Yeah. He wanted it behind the couch where the other kids were less likely to touch his Legos." That table had been moved several weeks earlier.

She looked at me, staring into my eyes for a few moments. "I really like where we are right now," she said.

I smiled. "Me too." I stepped to the bottom of the stairs close to her.

She leaned forward and fell into me. When I caught her, she gasped in a little wisp of pain. I was surprised it wasn't worse and shocked that she'd done this, considering how much she'd been hurting.

"You okay?" I asked.

"Yeah," she said. She surprised me again when she lifted her leg up against my hip. I reached around and grabbed her beneath her leg to support her, and then we did the same on the other side. Holding her up against me, I carried her back up the stairs. If this had been a Hollywood movie, this would have developed into a tender love scene. Instead, she winced and squeaked in pain continuously as we went up. At the top of the stairs, I started to let her down.

"No, it's okay," she said.

I rounded the corner and took a couple more steps across the room. We were at the end of our kitchen table.

"Okay, that's enough." She was digging her fingers into my upper back and wincing more in pain. I let her down slowly and gently. We had a high-top kitchen table with high chairs, and she was able to lean on the edge of the closest chair without having to stoop down. She took a few deep breaths as her face contorted with pain. So much for the love scene.

Thanks, cancer.

"Are you ever going to fix that cabinet door?"

The romance was too much to bear.

When the kids scrounged for snacks, they would climb the corner cabinet door onto the counter, ripping the hinges off. After fixing it three times in a few weeks, I set the door against the wall alongside the refrigerator, where it had remained for a few weeks. Actually, as I edit this over a year later, it is still leaning against the wall.

"I'll get right on that," I answered with all the enthusiasm I could muster.

"I won't hold my breath," she responded with equal vigor.

"Whatever, Christopher Walken hair," I shot back, cringing as her eyes widened and her jaw dropped. I'd never made any jokes about her losing her hair or how it looked growing back. She joked frequently, especially about the color, but I refrained. She had been dyeing her hair for so long—since before I knew her—that she hadn't seen her natural color in over two decades. It had grown back dark brown, far from the lighter shades I'd always seen.

The color was only part of it. It was growing back bushy, and the front swooped up in a way that made me think of a tidal wave rushing toward the shore. I had been aware for a few weeks that it reminded me of the way the actor Christopher Walken's hair typically looked. Until now, I hadn't spoken a word about this comparison. I don't mean to say anything derogatory about Christopher Walken's looks, but I don't think most women would be flattered having their looks compared to his in any way.

"HA! That's it!" Melanie cackled. "I've been trying to figure out what this mop looks like for weeks. It kept reminding me of something, but I couldn't place it! *That's it!*" She was delighted by my comparison, which relieved me greatly. "Wait, pull up a picture of him!"

My computer was on the table next to us. I found a perfect pic of him, in which his hair looked nearly identical to hers, and rotated the computer so she could see the screen better.

"YEEESSS!" she exclaimed. "That's *totally* it!"

We scrolled through a few more pictures of him, laughing hysterically.

"Wait. I need a mirror," she said, as giddy as ever, which was one of her trademarks I hadn't seen in quite some time. I hurried up the hall and grabbed her hand mirror off her dresser.

"It's a perfect match!" she exclaimed. "I should keep it this way!"

"Next time you go to get it done, just say, 'Give me the Walken,'" I told her, and we kept laughing like kids.

"Wait...is this the cowbell guy?" she asked. I knew exactly what she meant. Christopher Walken had done a skit on *Saturday Night Live* in which the cast, acting as the band Blue Oyster Cult, rehearsed a hard rock song called "(Don't Fear) The Reaper" that included the sounds of a cowbell. Walken repeatedly interrupted rehearsal, imploring the band, "I gotta have more cowbell!" The hilarious skit became incredibly popular, and I easily found a clip of it within seconds.

For the next twenty minutes or so, it was like the good old days again, a couple of giddy kids doing our best impersonations of Christopher Walken and laughing hysterically. We watched other *Saturday Night Live* skits and a couple movie clips featuring him. Neither of us could impersonate him worth a damn, but we couldn't have cared less about that. We were having a blast.

7

Mystery Episodes Explained

When Melanie said I wouldn't sign up for this again while walking the H in the hospital that day, I was annoyed. I felt I'd earned more than that. But then again, I certainly understood doubt in a marriage. I'd had bigger doubts than that.

"Oh, come on," she responded to my rolling eyes and shaking head. "You wouldn't get married again knowing it would come to this." I shook my head a little more and thought about what she said. We had just cried intensely together the day before. Didn't that show her how much I cared? Didn't that show her how much I loved her?

"I mean…you don't really believe that bullshit, do you?" I asked. "We have a great life. We've lived better than most people ever have."

"I know. You say that all the time."

"No, that's not what I mean," I shot back. I'm a private person—at least, I was until I decided to bare my soul in this book. I don't like public displays of affection, and I refrain from personal conversations in public places. I was reluctant to have this conversation in the hospital hallway, but we were engaged in it. I preferred to wait until we were back in her room, but at the rate she was moving, we weren't getting there soon.

Over the years, I had developed an appreciation for the awesome world we live in, particularly here in America today. It's not perfect and it has its problems, but it is extraordinary. I make an effort to appreciate it and count my blessings. Even through our financial struggles, I told Melanie this numerous times. Thanks to my business failing and other setbacks we'd experienced, along with some admittedly stupid decision-making, we lived about as poor as anyone we knew in our community and our circle of friends.

We both had master's degrees and years of professional experience. I worked in a lucrative industry as a software developer, and I even had a big, fancy title of Senior Software Engineer and Architect. Yet we were stuck in the 900-square-foot shoebox of a house that we had been in for over 18 years, and I still owed more in student loans than we owed on the house. There were six of us living in that house, and we only had one bathroom—not even another half-bath. We had almost no creature comforts or amenities. We didn't have a deck. We didn't have a patio. We didn't have a fireplace. We didn't have a pool or a hot tub. We didn't have a garage. We had small rooms with cheap furniture and cheaper fixtures. Our floors were worn down and our paint was faded and chipping. Neither of us had ever owned a new car or an expensive car. We didn't even have an ice maker.

By American standards today, we were not living large. At best, we were living about as basic and ordinary as it gets. Yet, whenever we got to discussing it, I would tell Melanie that I thought we lived better than most people have ever lived throughout history, and better than most people around the world likely live even today. We lived better than kings and queens, up until the last century or so. We had plumbing. We had electricity. We could refrigerate and freeze our food. We had the entire collection of human knowledge and experience at our fingertips on extraordinary computers. There was virtually unlimited entertainment at our fingertips using remote controls via satellite feeds and streaming services 24 hours a day. If we needed something, we could drive to any of a dozen stores around us within a few minutes and get practically anything we needed affordably. Advanced health care services were readily available. Even if the system has some serious flaws, it is still an almost incomprehensibly advanced system of care. Infections that would have killed most people within days in other places or times in human history have become minor nuisances to us—just go get a shot and maybe a prescription and forget about it.

I sincerely take these things to heart and appreciate them. These are extraordinary and awesome times we get to live in, although it's easy to lose perspective and take things for granted.

When Melanie responded that I say that all time, I wasn't referring to any of these blessings. I meant something else entirely.

"I don't mean the world we get to live in. I mean us. You're the best friend I've ever had." I faced her, looking her squarely in the eyes. "I love my life with you. I mean…sure, you're a pain in the ass sometimes, and we aren't perfect together, but who is? Do you think I think the grass is always greener? If I married someone else and not you, I would have just traded one set of problems for another, and I seriously doubt I would have had as much fun along the way. You're the most compassionate, kind, and extraordinary person I've ever known. If I had to go back and choose whether to marry you again, I wouldn't even hesitate, even knowing what a gimp you were going to end up."

She had tears welling in her eyes, but she was smiling. I think I had gotten through to her, maybe. I don't recall her saying anything. We shuffled up the hall as one of our friends showed up. We settled back into the room and chatted for a while with our visitor. Our little hospital hallway moment was over. At the time, I felt good about what I'd said to her. There would be plenty of chances in the coming months and years to continue this discussion. I'd make a better effort to show her how much I loved her. That's how I felt at the time. That's what I thought.

In my habit of naming significant events in my life, I dubbed this one The Epic Hallway Failure, and The Epic Hallway Failure would come back to haunt me.

Hospital staffers came and took Melanie for more tests. I found it somewhat curious that they were running tests today when they had planned to discharge her yesterday, but I was glad she was getting the attention and care she needed. I pulled out the cell phones and got busy once again on text messages and calls.

After I texted an update to cousin David, he called with more questions. Melanie's cousin David was a doctor, and he'd been our rock throughout Melanie's battle. He directed us to the Siteman Cancer Center, and we called him frequently with questions about her care. He understood the actions being taken and why they were being taken. We always felt better after talking to David. He answered our questions better than anyone, explaining issues and treatments clearly and reassuringly. Oddly, I didn't think to ask him about the mystery episodes, and I would wonder later why I didn't.

After I texted an update to Megan, she called with more questions. Megan was Melanie's first college roommate, and they remained close friends for life. Megan, a lawyer in New York, fired questions at me in random succession, like an attorney grilling a witness. I answered as best I could, but it was difficult to explain Melanie's complex medical issues, especially the mystery episodes.

"I'm coming in," Megan said. "I'll fly in tomorrow."

"No," I responded. "There's no need."

"Why not?" Megan prodded. "I can help with the kids. I can stay with Melanie when you aren't there."

"At some point, all that might help, but now isn't the time," I told her, before rattling off reasons. "The kids are covered. They're in school, and we have it worked out with family and friends to watch them. You would hardly see them. Melanie doesn't want visitors. She's embarrassed by her speech. Plus, she sleeps nearly 20 hours a day."

"Seriously?" Megan responded. "20 hours?"

"Yeah, they told me that's common after strokes. She needs rest and you wouldn't get to talk to her much. Like I said, we'd love to have you visit, but now isn't a good time."

"You're sure?" Megan said. "I don't mind. I'm happy to come and help. I want to come."

"I know," I told her. "And we want you to visit when the time is right, but... Hey, I'm gonna let you go. They're bringing Melanie back in from her tests."

"Okay, Paddy. Keep those updates coming, and let me know if I can do anything."

I talked to Melanie for a bit, and then she dozed off. About 30 minutes later, Dr. Gahlot came into the room. I had been hearing about Dr. Gahlot, one of Melanie's favorites. Apparently, their paths had crossed a few times during Melanie's care, although I had only seen her once before when she came in with the head doctor's entourage yesterday. We started talking, which woke Melanie. She gave a big smile when she saw the doc. Their familiarity was immediately clear, and they got chatty, even with Melanie's impaired speech. The discussion progressed to Dr. Gahlot's relationship status.

"Oh, I'm single," she said. Dr. Gahlot was attractive and young, probably mid-thirties. Her specialty was in neurology, so she was obviously very intelligent, well educated, and successful. She had a nice smile and a pleasant demeanor.

"Do you know Dr. Stewart?" Melanie asked her. The name sounded familiar to me, but I'd met so many. I didn't remember most of the doctors, and certainly not all their names.

"No..." Dr. Gahlot considered the question. "I don't know that name."

"He's a neurologist too. He works in the ER," Melanie told her. Her speech continued to be strained, but her statements were clear enough for us. "He's handsome and single!"

Dr. Gahlot smiled and laughed lightly. "No, I'm *aggressively* single," she said.

I suddenly remembered Dr. Stewart. I was stunned, not only by Melanie's current efforts, but even more by her previous efforts.

"Wait..." I interrupted. "When you were in the ER, having a stroke and barely able to speak, you were matchmaking back then, down there?"

Melanie gave me a look. She didn't like the interruption. She was on a mission, and she dismissed my question with a wave of her hand like she was swatting away an annoying insect.

I looked at Dr. Gahlot. "Did I just get waved off?"

Smiling broadly, Dr. Gahlot chuckled. I recalled Melanie talking to Dr. Stewart in the ER, the handsome young doctor who looked like he should be on a medical TV show, and I remembered how their conversation had seemed odd to me—and now I knew what she'd been up to.

"I was asked to come in and talk to you about your condition." Dr. Gahlot finally got to the purpose of her visit. She had brought in a cart with a computer and large monitor, and she wheeled it up to the foot of the bed.

"These are the most recent scans of your brain," she explained. The screen was divided into quadrants, with a picture from a scan of Melanie's brain from different angles in each quadrant. "This is the damage from your first stroke, the stroke that affected your vision." She pointed to a small oval-shaped area of discoloration. "As you can see, it isn't too large or too dark, as the damage was not extensive— fairly minor, as strokes go."

She continued explaining a few things about the Vision Stroke, and we listened attentively. She hit some keys on the keyboard, the screen flashed, and the pictures all changed. Before she said a word, I immediately noticed a huge difference.

"These scans show the area affected by the second stroke." She pointed to the image in the upper right quadrant of the screen, where there was clearly a much larger and much darker oval-shaped discoloration. I squirmed in my seat. "This shows the damaged area caused by your second stroke, which is what has affected your speech. We don't see any indications of any other strokes."

Dr. Gahlot explained how strokes could be, and frequently are, prolonged events. In Melanie's second stroke, a clot formed that blocked the blood vessel, causing her first episode in our shower while I was at the grocery store. As her episode transpired, blood building up behind the clot increased pressure until the blood finally burst through. As it did, it would take some pieces of the clot with it, beginning the process of breaking up the clot. However, most of the clot remained.

This resulted in a reduced opening that allowed some blood to pass, and during those intervals, Melanie would mostly seem okay. As more blood jammed behind the clot, some of it coagulated, temporarily choking off the flow of blood again and resulting in another episode. In Melanie's case, the second episode happened when we were in the cramped hospital room she'd been taken to from the ER. When the pressure built up again, the jammed blood burst through again, and the cycle continued. Each time the pressure built up and burst through the blockage, it would dislodge more bits of the clot and reduce its size, until eventually clearing the clot entirely.

Unfortunately, each cycle—what we'd been calling the mystery episodes—caused additional damage from the reduced blood flow to that area of her brain, which is why her speech kept getting worse and not coming back as well. The size and darkness of that oval spot on her scan increased with each cycle, providing us with visual confirmation to understand the mystery episodes.

FINALLY!

DAMN!

It made perfect sense, and it wasn't that hard to understand now that we'd had it explained to us. At least now, we knew what was happening and what we were dealing with, even if we still had myriad concerns about the future. This also made it clear why it's so important to get medical attention immediately if someone begins to have a stroke. Strokes can be more severe, such as when the clot is larger and restricts blood flow for longer periods. In such cases, the damage can be far worse. Based on observations during a patient's episodes and recovery intervals, medical professionals can evaluate whether more drastic measures need to be taken to clear the clot and avert more damage. These options are risky and not worth the consequences in less severe strokes, as they had initially recognized Melanie's to be. I now understood why the doctors and nurses had behaved as they did when observing Melanie suffering her stroke episodes, and similarly with my mom's seizures. While their seeming inaction frustrated me, they were making critical observations guided by their immense knowledge and expertise.

"So, let me see if I understand this correctly," I said to clarify. "All these episodes she's been having for two days have been the same stroke all along?"

"Yes, that's exactly right," Dr. Gahlot confirmed. "The scans show no indication of any other stroke activity, other than the first stroke she had that affected her vision." Dr. Gahlot then explained how our brains are compartmentalized. I don't recall the numbers, but she explained that there are thousands, or maybe it was millions, of blood vessels supplying blood to the brain. If you could stretch them out end to end, these little blood vessels would collectively span thousands of miles. Due to the compartmentalization of our brains, a clot in any given vessel only causes damage in an isolated area of the brain. The rest of the brain continues to function unaffected. These explanations fascinated me. I gained a far greater appreciation for what a marvel our brains are and what a brilliant design they have. Our minds are almost incapable of comprehending our brains. Our discussion was now easily over 30 minutes long, and we weren't close to being done yet.

"I'm sorry, this isn't directed at you," I said to Dr. Gahlot. "I appreciate your time and your explanation, which has been excellent. But why in the hell couldn't someone explain this to us two days ago, or even yesterday? Even if no one gave us this detailed of an explanation, just to tell us this was all still the same stroke and that it's a prolonged event would have helped! I mean...with all the highly educated medical professionals running around, how did not one of you understand what we meant when we were asking about these episodes? I think you all need some classes or recurring training on how to talk like normal people and drop all the Latin terms and medical jargon when you're talking to patients."

This a pet peeve of mine, and the tech geeks in my profession are just as bad as medical professionals. I was always able to explain complex things in plain language, and I never understood why it was so hard for others to do so. Not only would I have been annoyed by this lack of simple communication in any other circumstance, it was infuriating while trying to cope with this life-threatening series of mystery episodes for days. Is it really that hard to think and talk like a normal person, or understand the concerns of someone who asks normal questions?

Maybe it's just me.

However, I'm compelled to point out the admiration I have for modern medical science in general and the care Melanie received throughout all this. These medical professionals were brilliant and professional from the beginning. I'm grateful for all the care they gave Melanie, and I'm confident in them, but they're human beings and they aren't perfect, which is okay. I just wish they could have saved us a lot of stress and grief and explained the basics of what was happening much sooner. Maybe I should have looked up more online or called someone else, like cousin David. *Why didn't I call cousin David?* I guess I placed my faith in those who were providing Melanie the care; I am confident they were doing the best that could be done overall.

I glanced at Melanie, and she was giving me that look. I would sometimes joke that Melanie reminded me of Hannibal Lecter. If you aren't familiar with the books or the movies, Hannibal Lecter is a character in a series of stories about serial killers. Dr. Hannibal Lecter was a psychiatrist, and he loved to get inside people's heads. He would interrogate people, trying to learn their darkest secrets and fears. It gave him great satisfaction when he got them to admit things or tell him things they would normally keep buried inside. Hannibal also hated rudeness, which was also like Melanie. While she would be so kind and compassionate to most people she met, she couldn't stand assholes and wouldn't hesitate to call bullshit on anything.

I would joke that Melanie was like Hannibal Lecter except that she wouldn't kill you and eat you if she didn't like you, as Hannibal the Cannibal did in the stories. He only killed and ate rude or dis-courteous people. Over the years, I quit making that joke as some people found it weird and not really funny. So, instead of Hannibal the Cannibal references, I've gone on thinking of Melanie as my Yoda—my little Jedi Master of relationships.

When Melanie gave me the look, it felt more Hannibal than Yoda. I didn't want to be dinner. She would be especially displeased since Dr. Gahlot was one of her favorites. She adored the doc.

"I'm sorry, doc," I said. "Again, we really do appreciate your time and your explanation. It has really been helpful—tremendous! Thank you so much for doing this."

Dr. Gahlot said she understood my frustrations and even agreed with me, which made me feel validated. More importantly, I was relieved since I figured it got me off the hook with my personal Dr. Lecter for my little soapbox rant. The conversation among us remained cordial and friendly, so dinner would be coming from the cafeteria as usual tonight.

"So, what's the prognosis?" I asked. "What can we expect moving forward?"

"There's a good chance she can recover most of her speech, maybe entirely, but I don't want to get your hopes up. She will need speech therapy, and the speech therapists can evaluate her and give you a better idea of what to expect in that regard."

"Really?" I said. I was surprised to hear that she could recover that completely. It would be wonderful, but I was weary of getting Melanie's hopes up. Seeing that scan that revealed the damage, on top of watching Melanie's struggles, made me skeptical no matter how much I wanted to believe it. "So that damage will repair itself? Is it like a bruise that will fade away over time?"

"No, it doesn't work like that," Dr. Gahlot responded. "We only use a small percentage of our brain." The notion that we use only a small percentage of our brains is something I've heard many times in my life, often with the suggestion that our brains may contain supernatural abilities. In movies and books, characters could tap into these abilities to move objects with their minds or engage in telepathy. These possibilities are exciting to imagine.

As Dr. Gahlot explained the capacity for recovery, I began to comprehend a different scenario. Because of my work in the realm of computers and IT, I could relate to what she was explaining quite easily. The brain is like a computer in many ways. We only use a small percentage of our brains in the same way that a computer typically uses only a percentage of its processing power or memory and storage capacity. For example, as Dr. Gahlot explained, there's an area of the brain that controls speech and communication, which was damaged in Melanie's brain. There is ample unused tissue in that area of the brain, and that unused tissue can take over for the damaged area. Depending on the extent of the damage, this can happen quickly or take an extended time. It would require prolonged recovery when the damage is greater because the unused tissue has to be developed or trained just as the damaged area was originally. If there is extensive damage in a given area, the extent of recovery may be more limited. There are many factors that play into all this, and even with all we have learned, there is still much we don't know.

The tissue in any given area of the brain is designed and dedicated to its own functions, just as the storage of a smart phone can't be used for anything other than storage. Even though we only use a small percentage of our brains, the tissue we don't use is still devoted to its given function. We can't magically gain clairvoyance because we have extra unused tissue in the region of our brain that controls vision or speech. However, if we have damage, even later in life, we have reserve tissue that can enable us to recover from traumatic events, such as strokes. This is also why you can teach an old dog new tricks. If you are in your seventies and you want to learn to play the piano, you can because you have spare brain tissue that can be trained to do so.

As a result of this new information we learned from our session with Dr. Gahlot, which had now taken well over an hour, we had a renewed sense of hope and a far greater understanding of everything that was happening to Melanie. With her terrific personality, professionalism, knowledge, friendliness, and her ability to communicate so well, I could see why Melanie liked the doc so much.

"So, what does our daily life look like moving forward?" I asked.

"Well…she'll be going to therapy for likely at least a few months—occupational therapy, physical therapy, and speech therapy—but we'll know more after they do evaluations. We will give you a list of providers, and you can pick one near you to schedule her evaluations. And she'll be on blood thinner medications indefinitely. We're still working through which one we'll prescribe and the dosage."

I asked more about the blood thinners, and Dr. Gahlot explained that there are multiple drugs that can thin the blood to varying degrees of thickness and for longer or shorter durations, and with each one, there are considerations of the dosage. With Melanie on so many different drugs, including chemo, and her other myriad health issues, the selection of which blood thinner and dosage was a complex decision. Although these developments indicated deteriorations in her condition, with strokes, additional medications, and therapy, I took an optimistic outlook. They identified the causes. They had plans. They had actionable ideas.

We discussed that with therapy, Melanie might be better overall in several months than she was before the stroke. Along with restoring speech and vision, therapy might even strengthen her back and help her walk better than she had for over a year. I was cautiously optimistic. Things were looking up. Dr. Gahlot also mentioned that Melanie should be able to resume chemo soon so we could get back to combatting the liver tumor and keeping the cancer under control. I was back to thinking that I'd still have at least a few more years with Melanie, and maybe they would find better treatments or a cure during that time and prolong her time with us even more. Maybe I'd still get to sing the Beatles' "When I'm Sixty-Four" to her when I turned 64, and maybe Paul McCartney's "Maybe I'm Amazed" right along with it. A dork can dream. There was hope.

"So, what do you think? Once we finalize our decision on the blood thinner medication, are you comfortable with being discharged now?" Dr. Gahlot asked.

"Uh...NO!" Melanie facetiously exclaimed. She struggled with the words, but we clearly understood, "Only if you come with us!"

When we quit laughing, we thanked Dr. Gahlot again and she left. Later that day, Melanie was discharged. By the time I pulled the car around to the pickup area, a staffer had wheeled her down. Despite the impaired speech, they were talking and laughing like old friends.

Melanie. Only Melanie.

8

Rebound and Relapse

It was a warm, sunny day when Melanie was discharged. It felt good to be back out in the open air under the blue sky with her, even if it was only the short walk to the car in front of the hospital. She was exhausted. I asked if she wanted to get something to eat, but she was too tired, even for drive-thru. She went to bed when we got home. I had to wake her up every few hours to take her meds, especially the blood thinners. The blood thinners were given as an injection in her belly, which she insisted on doing herself. It didn't seem to bother her. I don't think I could stick a needle in my own belly, but she did it almost nonchalantly as if she'd been doing it her entire life.

Even though she was exhausted, she came out and sat on the sofa with the kids, who were thrilled to see her. The younger ones climbed all over her. She deliberately asked short questions, and her ability to control her speech surprised me. It was the only time she could. She spoke slowly, but her concerted efforts made her speech sound mostly normal for the kids. The kids commented that she talked funny, but they didn't appear upset by it. It was such a joy to see her snuggling and interacting with the kids again.

The next week was a lesson in community. The support and generosity we received were overwhelming. I'd individually acknowledge everyone, but that would take dozens of pages. People helped with the kids, brought food, sent cards and gift cards, and more. Multiple times per day I would find meals, snacks, desserts, groceries, supplies, games, toys, and more on our porch. Yard work mysteriously got done. A laundry service arrived unexpectedly. I can't recall everything people did—much of it anonymously, so I didn't even know whom to thank. I was amazed how people thought of things that were awesomely helpful or fun, but I never would have thought to do for someone. It was overwhelming and humbling, and I will be eternally grateful.

Melanie was sleeping nearly 20 hours per day, and after a couple days, my concern grew. I searched for answers briefly online and then contacted her doctor. This was apparently not unusual for someone recovering from a stroke, and I learned it could continue for some time. I worked from home, took care of the kids, and woke Melanie periodically to take meds. Each evening, she would come out for an hour or so and hang out with the kids, but then she went right back to sleep. Despite being with her around-the-clock, I hardly spoke to her.

On the following Wednesday, I took her to OT, PT, and speech evaluations. She was a hit. The therapists and other patients loved her, and we were laughing and joking with everyone. I accompanied her during evaluations. The OT and PT tests were distressing, as she performed surprisingly poorly on some of their exercises. Nevertheless, the therapists were optimistic about her recovery, and that was the most important part.

The speech evaluation was the most daunting. Despite my anxiety about how that evaluation would go, it was fun. Melanie cracked jokes as we answered their questions and joked more during the exercises. At one point, Melanie cracked a joke and the therapist exclaimed, "I can't wait to work with you! We're going to get along great!"

Everywhere she went.

The speech evaluation came last. The other therapists formulated their treatment plans during that session. When speech was done, the therapist spent a couple minutes on her computer, then the full schedule was ready.

"Okay, so you'll come in every day, Monday through Friday, for the next six weeks," the speech therapist began. "Sorry, these will be long days. You'll need to bring a lunch. After that, OT and PT will evaluate you again and determine how much longer they need you to keep coming. Most likely, those will continue, but only three days a week after that." She pulled a piece of paper off the printer. "We have a courtesy van that can pick you up and bring you home each day if you need that, but we need to know if you want to use the van right away because we need to get you on the pickup schedule."

"Wait," I said. "What about speech? You said OT and PT will reevaluate. Will speech continue three days a week without another evaluation, or what is the plan for that?"

"No," the therapist responded, "we'll be done with speech. We already got approval for six weeks with your insurance, and we don't expect to do any more than that."

"Because insurance won't cover it?" I asked. That wasn't acceptable. If Melanie needed more therapy, we weren't going to stop because insurance wouldn't cover it. She cared about speaking well more than walking well—or anything else. She lived for people and relationships. She couldn't interrogate people if she couldn't speak. She *had* to talk to her kids. Talking was the core of her existence. If any of these therapies were cut short, it would *not* be speech. "Look, if we have to pay for it ourselves, we will, but we aren't stopping because of insurance."

"No, no! Sorry!" the therapist exclaimed. "I'm sorry! I should have clarified that better. We don't expect her to need any more than the six weeks."

I thought over these words. I dreaded asking a question or getting an answer that would upset Melanie, but we had to be clear on this.

"You don't expect her to need more than six weeks be-cuuuzzz…" I paused for a response, but the therapist looked puzzled. "How well do you expect her speech to recover?" I clarified. "How well do you think she'll be speaking when you're done?"

"Oh!" the therapist responded. "We expect full recovery."

Those words hung in the air momentarily. I looked at Melanie, and I felt the same look on my face that she had on hers. I wanted to be elated. I wanted to believe, but I couldn't help but thinking we were misunderstanding something.

"In the hospital, they told us that she would be recovering for a year, and even then, she might not recover fully, but you're telling us that you think she will be completely back to speaking normally in *six weeks*?"

"Yes," the therapist replied. "I've had patients much older than her with greater loss of speech recover in about the same time frame. I don't see any reason to think that she won't do better. She certainly is motivated, and that makes a big difference."

I looked at Melanie again, and once again thought we shared the same feelings. She had a slight smile but with obviously reserved doubt. We wanted to believe, and we wanted to be joyful, but what if this young therapist was wrong? Sometimes hope can be scary, even dangerous.

The next week went well, but it was a struggle. To maximize time and take care of the kids, I worked from home, but we decided to have Melanie ride the courtesy van. It was like having a fifth kid. It was a chore waking her up for blood thinner injections or any other reason. She slept an excessive amount, although her sleep hours were limited due to therapy. She continued to spend an hour or so with the kids each evening but went right back to bed afterward. I had to make my fifth kid her lunch each day and help her get dressed. And yet, with all that, it was awesome having her home, and she was working her way back to health. If that therapist was right, we'd be back to having full and smooth conversations soon, and she might be walking better and driving soon. Ever since The Escape Clause Revelation, I appreciated it all exponentially more.

By the end of the week, we noticed something that prodigiously boosted our hopes. We hadn't detected improvement in her speech during the week, but it must have been gradually improving. Near the end of the week, we were talking in the evening, and she said a few sentences in an evidently quicker cadence and struggled with individual words noticeably less. That six-week prediction was starting to seem believable.

During that same week, she visited her oncologist, who was also acting as her primary care physician. They determined she was ready to resume chemo as all her vitals were good. She was getting her speech back, getting stronger, and now would be getting back to the battle to defeat the cancer that was still lurking within. She was fighting on multiple fronts, as she always had. I could feel the rebound happening. She'd be speaking soon, driving in weeks, and walking well in months. This was why I kept a positive outlook.

Suck it, Trebek!

The following Monday, Stephanie took her to the chemo appointment. Sometime around eleven o'clock that morning, I received a text from Steph. They weren't doing chemo and were readmitting her to the hospital for observation due to Melanie's complaints of leg pain.

Damn! What leg pain? She didn't complain of that the night before or this morning. I called Steph immediately.

"Hold on…" Steph said. I said nothing and held on as requested.

"Are you there?" she finally asked.

"Yes," I acknowledged.

"Okay, just a minute…" Steph said. I heard muffled voices in the background. No one sounded panicked, and then it got quiet.

"Okay," Steph was back on the line. "Sorry, they just took her out of the room to run tests."

"She's having leg pain?" I asked. "Did she say when that started? She wasn't complaining last night or this morning, and she was moving as well as she has been when she left the house."

"It seems to have started after we got to the hospital. That's what she told the doctors when they asked her," Steph explained. "They were getting her prepped for chemo when she first brought it up, and then she complained of trouble breathing. She wanted to get something to eat on the way in, which seemed like a good sign that she had an appetite, but then she barely ate."

"So…" I hesitated. I was afraid to utter the word *stroke*. "This is more precautionary? Nothing worse is happening?"

"Seems that way. The leg pain and shortness of breath concerned them enough to put a halt on chemo and check her out."

Steph and I talked a little more, and then I told her to call me as soon as they learned anything new, which she would have done anyway, of course.

Hours passed before Steph called again. She was with the doctor and put us on speaker phone so I could hear the doctor's brief with them.

"The clotting has spread," the doctor began.

"What does that mean?" I immediately asked. What clot would spread? I thought she didn't have any more clots. "Did a clot get bigger, or is this a new clot, or what are we talking about?"

"Well, she has multiple small clots in her lung, which explains the trouble breathing, and she has three clots in her leg."

We were all silent for a few moments. This terrified me. If multiple clots formed while she was on blood thinners, did that mean they couldn't stop the clotting? Was this simply out of control now? I wanted to shout these questions out, but I didn't want to stir panic. I was on Steph's speaker phone, which meant Melanie could hear anything I said.

"How can that happen when she's on blood thinners?" I asked as calmly as I could.

"Well, we might need to adjust the dosage," the doctor responded. "Two shots per day may not be enough. It's also possible she's having an allergic reaction, and we might need to switch to a different blood thinner. That's not uncommon. We're checking her platelet count. A low platelet count can cause the blood to thicken and then clot more easily. We're going to keep running tests and scan her other leg and her chest. We'll keep her overnight for observation."

I'd learned to appreciate longer explanations with multiple potential problems. In the past, it might have freaked me out that so many things could be going wrong, but I'd come to welcome these multifactored possibilities. Somehow, long explanations made me feel like the doctors knew what they were doing—they knew what to look for and that they had courses of action to take. If they could identify a problem and isolate its sources, I believed they would solve it. This relieved me—somewhat. If they didn't have ideas or courses of actions, that would terrify me. Fortunately, as they had from the beginning when she was initially diagnosed, they had ideas and plans and courses of action. That's what I wanted to hear.

The doctor also mentioned they could implant a filter in her belly, a device that apparently could help prevent clotting. It didn't make much sense to me. I couldn't imagine how a filter in her belly would prevent clots in other areas of her body, especially her brain, which was the scariest possibility. But they still had ideas, plans, and courses of actions, so I kept on trusting that the doctors knew what they were doing, and I kept the faith. Besides, he said the filter was only a possibility depending on the results of the tests, and they wouldn't even start considering it before tomorrow. My guess was he wanted to introduce the idea so it would be less shocking if it came up later in a more urgent situation.

I also asked why Melanie's platelet count could be low. What caused that? He didn't know. Apparently, there can be many reasons for that to happen. They would need to run tests to determine, which was another reason they were readmitting her, yet again, and keeping her in the hospital for at least another day or two.

I called my sister Liz and told her what was happening and what we knew. She lived about a mile from us, and she offered to watch the kids after school so I could get to the hospital. Melanie adored Liz and her family, and our kids were always thrilled to play with their cousins. Melanie would be glad to know the kids were with them. Back on the road to the hospital, I stopped for his-and-her fountains on the way. When I got to the hospital, Steph was still there, but Melanie was not.

"They're running more tests on her," Steph informed me after hellos and a hug. In the old days, I would have asked what tests, but I'd learned it didn't matter. I couldn't keep track of all the damn tests. What mattered were the results, so I waited for the doctors to come with the results and the plans. It was all about the plans and the prognosis.

In this double-occupancy room, there were two chairs but no other occupant. We were sitting alone, about the width of Melanie's missing hospital bed apart with nothing but empty floor between us.

"How are you holding up?" I asked Steph. It had been a long day for her.

"I don't know," she said flatly. Suddenly, I could see tears welling up in her eyes. "When I brought her in this morning, I pulled up to the front of the hospital. She said she was okay walking in, so I stayed in the car to go park. She walked around the front of the car, and she looked and moved like a 90-year-old woman. She didn't even look like my sister!"

Stephanie dropped her head into her hands for a moment then lifted her head as she took a deep breath.

"And then I came back into the room a little while ago and Melanie was sleeping in the bed. She looked exactly like my mom did the last time I visited her in the hospital." Steph was 12 when their mom died from breast cancer. Steph put her hands on her face and cried a little, but she was holding it together.

"You know, I'm not going to silver-line you," I said, and Steph smiled at that one. That was Melanie's line. Melanie had a pragmatic approach to her condition. She didn't like false positivity, and if you tried to feed her mega-optimism, you would get admonished with the line, "*Don't silver-line me!*"

"Truth is," I continued, "Melanie could have a massive clot and a massive stroke and be gone any minute, but medicine has drastically improved in these last few decades since your mom went through this. The doctors know much more and have better ways of treating things now, and they are still working it. They aren't out of ideas or plans." I paused to think about what I was saying, not entirely sure I believed it myself, but I wanted to. "I was thinking about these new clots today. It's scary that she's still clotting and has multiple clots, but the doctor also said they were small clots. It seems the blood thinners are working. This would likely be much worse without the blood thinners. Now they figure out the right blood thinner med to use and the dosage. As long as they know the problem and have plans of action, they can deal with it. When they run out of ideas, that's when we'll be screwed, but that hasn't happened yet. They're getting her through this."

"Right." Steph nodded. "That's exactly what David told me once. I need to keep that in mind."

She seemed encouraged, somewhat, by that. I think I might have even encouraged myself. I think I even believed myself a little bit.

Melanie stayed in the room until the next day, and the tests seemed nonstop, then they decided to transfer her. She had remained at the location where she had come for chemo but was moving to the main campus with more testing facilities and personnel. Barnes Hospital and the Siteman Cancer Center had multiple locations, so an ambulance was needed for the long drive. Out in front of the hospital, I once again stood behind an ambulance and looked through the little square window at her. She once again blew me a kiss before the ambulance pulled off.

The doctor had explained to me that the floor they were transferring her to was sort of an intensive care unit, but not *the* intensive care unit. That meant there were more staff dedicated to each patient to provide continuous coverage, but it wasn't as restrictive as the full-blown ICU. It was pseudo-ICU. I pseudo-understood what the hell he meant by pseudo-ICU, but I didn't need to understand nor did I care. I was just happy they were working through the problems.

When I got to the room, Melanie was already situated, and a nurse was hooking her up to her new wires and tubes and the beeping and buzzing and dinging and hissing and humming machines. The room was huge and obviously much newer than any other room we had been in. It was single occupancy, which was a surprise considering how big it was. It had large sliding glass doors to the bathroom with an expansive open shower. Oddly, I couldn't help feeling like I was in a resort hotel room—almost. It reminded me of the room we had on our honeymoon—sort of.

When everything was hooked up, the nurse began drawing blood. She explained some of the additional blood tests that had been ordered. While I knew there was a lot that could be detected from blood, I was learning that extensively more could be determined by running specific tests. However, each test required more blood, so the nurse drew a few vials for this round of tests. The major concern was still Melanie's decreasing platelet count, and they were scrambling to try to figure out what was causing it.

The next couple days crept by in the most uneventful series of hectic and incessant action I have ever encountered. An unceasing procession of medical health professionals streamed in and out with explanations and updates—mostly about how they didn't know anything new. It was chaos, and yet it felt as if nothing was happening. They eliminated some possibilities, but her low platelet count stumped them. Wednesday felt like Tuesday, except when I thought it was Thursday, or sometimes Tuesday, and Thursday seemed to be

Wednesday except for times when I couldn't comprehend what day it was, or if it even was a day. Melanie was back to sleeping about 20 hours a day, which the doctors and nurses still assured me was normal poststroke, as abnormal as it seemed.

Several visitors came and went, and those were nice visits. At least one of them commented that the room looked like a resort room, making me feel oddly validated in my assessment. Later, I sat there wondering why I needed to feel validated for having that opinion. I guess I had nothing else to think about, or I had too much to think about, or I didn't want to think about what I had to think about. I think that was on Wednesday, or Thursday, or maybe Tuesday. Or maybe I thought about it on each of those days. Then I couldn't even remember if we were in this room on Tuesday, or if we didn't get here until Wednesday.

I clearly remember when it was Thursday because a hospital worker entered and handed me some papers. She wasn't a nurse or a doctor; she held some sort of administrative position. "This is a power-of-attorney form and a medical directive form that we recommend you fill out. We don't have one on file for Melanie."

"Do we need that?" I asked hesitantly.

"We prefer that patients in this ward have these documents on file, although it isn't required," she said, fortunately without conveying a sense of urgency. Yet, I wondered, *why now?* We had been in this room for a couple days, so why didn't they present these to us on arrival or yesterday?

"We'll look at those later," I said. Melanie's eyes were drooping. We weren't at a point where we needed such documents anyway.

"Those will need to be notarized," the administrator commented as I dropped the papers on the table next to me. "We have a notary on staff who can come here to the room when you have the forms completed."

I nodded. We could always look at those later. Policy is policy, but I was sure we didn't need them.

When Melanie woke up, she was more alert than she had been in days. We talked about the forms, deciding to go ahead and fill them out. If we waited until some day when we weren't in the hospital, we'd have to make a special trip to a notary and pay a fee. It would be easier to do it now and have the documents on file. We didn't need them, but we had nothing better to do. We filled them out, and the staff did the rest. The notary even made extra copies for us. I'd throw them in our file cabinet and forget about them. Formalities, policies, nothing more.

I stepped out to the family room. Melanie's resort room was the last patient room near the end of the hallway. A waiting room at the end of the hallway was denoted by a sign that said, "Family Room." The corner room had glass outer walls on two sides. The door to the Family Room was adjacent to the door to Melanie's room, making it quick and easy for me to utilize it.

The Family Room had a beautiful view of St. Louis's expansive Forest Park. Every year in October, the American Cancer Society hosted the Making Strides Walk in Forest Park to raise awareness and fundraise to fight breast cancer. Our family had been participating in it since Melanie's breast cancer diagnosis three and a half years earlier. Forest Park is a huge urban park, spanning 1,300 acres and home to multiple museums, multiple golf courses, multiple ball fields, a zoo, an amphitheater, walking paths, and more. Looking out the floor-to-ceiling window overlooking the park, I could see the pathways the Making Strides Walk followed each year.

I decided to call Megan, Melanie's college roommate. Since she practically bought a plane ticket while I was on the phone with her days ago, I knew she wanted to visit. With Melanie in the pseudo-ICU, I was expecting a long weekend and maybe a longer week. While other family and friends were happy to help, it would be nice to have someone so close to Melanie who could focus solely on her, without local distractions or obligations.

"Hey, girl, how are you feeling?" Megan answered. I'd called her from Melanie's phone since I didn't have Megan's number in my phone. She had obviously seen Melanie's name on the caller ID.

"It's Patrick." Although I felt like I knew Megan pretty well, it struck me how little I had ever talked directly to her. We communicated almost exclusively through Melanie's relayed comments during phone conversations. She probably knew more about me than I would have wanted her to know, as Melanie certainly had vented to Megan many times about me. However, as soon as I talked to Megan, it was immediately like I was talking to my own sister.

"Oh, hey dude, what's up?" I could hear the apprehension in her voice.

"There's nothing really new to report," I reported. "They're still running tests and working the problems."

"Okay…" she said in a clearly concerned and cautious tone.

"I think this weekend would be a good time to come visit, if you still want to."

The line was silent for a bit.

"Dude, just tell me straight up, is it time to say goodbye?" she asked.

"No, sorry, I didn't mean to alarm you like that. I mean…I can't tell you that things aren't bad, but we aren't thinking…that." I contemplated what to say next, realizing I hadn't thought through what I'd been saying up to this point. "I don't know... We're kind of in a whole new realm here."

"What does that mean?" she asked. I couldn't blame her for asking. That was a pretty damn generic statement.

"Even with the blood thinners, she's still clotting," I explained. "They've moved her to another unit where she gets more attention."

"ICU?" Megan asked.

"No." I didn't want to explain the whole pseudo-ICU thing that I didn't even understand. "She's in a unit with dedicated nurses so she gets more attention, but it isn't ICU."

Megan kept firing questions, and I explained the low platelet count, possible allergic reaction to the blood thinner, and additional blood tests as best I could. With each question I answered, the answers only led to more questions, so the conversation with Megan was a nearly perfect echo of the overall situation.

"You know, Megan, I don't know," I finally said. The lawyer, almost predictably, had been direct and forceful with her questions. As a younger man, I might have taken offense and felt like she was judging and criticizing me, but now I took it in stride. What I heard wasn't judgment; it was her love and concern for Melanie.

"Look," I continued, "I haven't been told anything that indicates it's time to say goodbye. We aren't there. That isn't why I'm telling you to come in now. They could get Melanie stabilized, and she could still be with us for the next five or ten years. And who knows, maybe they'll find better treatments or a cure by then and we'll grow old together. I just don't know." I paused to switch gears and think about what to say next. "The risk factors have increased substantially. We will, for at least a while, be living with a constant fear of her having a clot, which could cause a stroke at any moment. I suppose you could say that could happen to anyone at any time, but she is high-risk for it for specific medical reasons, and right now, they aren't sure why, but they're working like crazy to figure it out. I trust the doctors. We're in one of the best cancer treatments centers in the world. There isn't anywhere else I would want her to be right now to fight this shit. I can't remember or explain all the medical explanations I've heard for days and weeks now, but I have to trust the doctors. It is what it is."

After a short pause, Megan said, "I get it, dude." Megan got online to book a flight for the next day as we continued talking. "I need to wrap some things up so I can get out of here. I'll see you tomorrow."

It seemed eerily quiet as soon as we hung up. I sat silently in the Family Room staring down at Forest Park and the pathways of the Making Strides Walk, illuminated by the rays of the setting sun. I pictured walking with Melanie once again this coming October in a huge pack of our friends and family. I tried to think of Melanie standing tall and walking better, imagining therapy had made her stronger. I could see us on that path.

The remainder of Thursday was mostly filled with tests and texts. Melanie slept most of the time, and a few visitors came by. Tiffani and others came in the evening and were staying late, so I headed home once again to be with the kids. I slept fitfully, and Thursday rolled into Friday. The kids were off to school, and I was back on the road, stopping for his-and-her fountains before making my way into Melanie's hospital resort room. The first couple hours conformed to our new ordinary. Melanie slept a lot, and I helped her to the bathroom once.

The nurse entered the room with a cart and pushed it bedside. She lifted a tray with a container of at least a dozen vials. I watched as she started drawing blood and filling a vial—another ordinary activity at the resort. She filled another vial, then another, and another—and just kept filling.

I shifted in my chair. Something was wrong. This wasn't good. It felt desperate. They didn't have a clue what was happening. They were grasping at straws now.

"Don't jump to conclusions," I told myself. Maybe this was good. This meant they still had ideas. They were still working the problems. As long as they had actionable ideas and plans, they were still driving at solutions.

"Why are you drawing so much blood?" I finally asked. She had filled almost all the vials yet was still drawing blood.

"Well…" She was cautious and hesitant, like she was choosing her words carefully, and that scared me. The anxious look on her face terrified me. She didn't want to answer, and that in itself was an answer—an answer I didn't want. "The doctors want to run additional tests to look for some specific indicators."

"What are they looking for, specifically?" I asked.

She hesitated again—not good.

"The main thing they are concerned about is her liver function."

Although they had already mentioned concerns about her liver, the concerns didn't seem immediate or critical. This was different. There was something ominous about this. Before it appeared to be one thing on a list of many to explore, but now it seemed like the focal point. I'd spent enough time in hospitals to differentiate the routine from the red flag. At least a dozen dark red vials, which had recently been clear, sat on the tray. Boredom and disorientation vanished, replaced by acute fixation and anxiety. This was certainly going to be a long weekend. I was even more grateful that Megan was coming in now.

"How long will it take to get the results of these tests?" I asked the nurse.

"A couple hours," she said. "They're putting a priority on these tests. Depending on the results, they're weighing if they will do a biopsy on her liver. They're considering that for tomorrow morning."

Priority. Biopsy. Liver.

DAMN!

"Can they do that while she's on blood thinners?" I asked. A biopsy on her liver would be an invasive surgery, and any invasive surgery with incisions that would cause bleeding would be dangerous for a patient on blood thinners. Plus, it was her liver, and if their concerns were serious enough to consider a biopsy…

Considering the clotting and…

If her liver was causing…

DAMN!

"Yes, that's an issue. It gets complicated, but that's one of the reasons for all these tests." The nurse gestured at the vials. I glanced from the vials to the notarized forms on the table next to my chair.

I asked her a few more questions, but I knew my discussion with the nurse wouldn't change anything. I didn't want to keep her from getting that blood delivered for the tests, so I pulled back and left it to the professionals. I can't say I ever got used to feeling helpless, but I had certainly adapted to conducting myself as a powerless participant when appropriate to do so.

The doctor entered the room less than two hours later. They weren't kidding about expediting those tests. We woke Melanie up.

"Based on the test results, we're concerned about diminished liver function," the doctor informed us.

"Oh, great," Melanie groaned. She fell back against her pillow. Melanie had always been an engaged and informed patient. She took copious notes throughout her care, interrogated her doctors, researched, and consulted with David and others. She was acutely aware of the significance of liver function and the threat of her tumor.

"We want to move forward with a biopsy of the liver," the doctor continued before I could ask what the next steps would be. "It will be tricky to get her numbers where we need them for surgery."

In the ensuing explanation, the catch-22s were plentiful. They needed to take her off the blood thinners, mostly if not entirely. The numbers indicated how thinned her blood was, and they were watching those numbers intently. The first problem was that as her blood regained thickness, the risk of clotting increased. They needed her off blood thinners for surgery, but they couldn't risk taking her off blood thinners.

That was only the beginning of the problems. I can't remember half of what we were being told. I didn't want to waste the precious time they had. The number of things that could go wrong was staggering and overwhelming.

Shut up.

Let them do their jobs.

Trust them and leave them alone.

They were still fighting.

They still had plans.

They still had actionable ideas.

Melanie fell back asleep before the doctor finished her full explanation. I was shocked she could fall asleep, regardless of how exhausted she was.

Was she checking out?

She couldn't. She was too strong for that.

For the first time, this started to feel like it did when my dad passed away fourteen years earlier. That was my only direct experience with death. My dad had an aortic aneurism when I was at Parks College. An aortic aneurism is a tear in the aorta itself, which is the main artery of the body stemming from the heart. He began to feel back pain while raking leaves and went inside to lay down. He ended up going to the hospital soon after, and it was a life-saving decision. The doctors said he would have internally bled to death within about three hours. They operated and replaced his aorta, which was later explained to be a reinforcement, technically speaking. Either way, my respect and awe of modern medical science and the skills and genius of medical professionals increased exponentially that day. I couldn't imagine how they could replace or reinforce the aorta. I still marvel at that.

I got 11 more years with my dad because of that miracle surgery, and it was 11 years I am eternally grateful to have shared with him. What a gift. With declining health, including emphysema in his lungs and multiple other health problems, mainly brought on by decades of smoking, he suffered additional aortic aneurisms 11 years later. The doctors tried to stabilize him so he might be able to survive another replacement surgery, but they finally decided surgery was not an option.

My dad had been awake, alert, and talking while we awaited the doctors' decision, but his body gave out shortly after the doctor delivered the news. I watched it happen. I was standing at the foot of his bed as his eyes rolled back and closed, and he drifted into unconsciousness. I don't believe in ghosts or a lot of spiritual mumbo jumbo. I would not have believed our minds could have that much conscious control of the internal workings of our bodies, but my dad proved to me that we can. He showed the will to fight and sustain his life as long as he had some measure of hope. He was fighting with his full strength and resolve. He willed himself to remain alive until the doctors told him it was done, and then his body let go, and he drifted away over the next few hours. He fought until the fight was taken from him.

I walked to Melanie's side. With one hand, I grasped her hand, and I placed my other hand on her forehead as I leaned in. "Hey," I said softly.

She squeezed my hand and opened her eyes. She was still in the fight.

"Hey," she mumbled. She opened her eyes briefly and gave me a slight smile.

"You're the Grest," I said.

"*You're* the Grest," she responded then closed her eyes and fell back asleep.

The Grest was our highest compliment to each other. We created it in our first year of marriage. She told me one day that I was great. I intended to respond by elevating "great" to "the best," but the words got jumbled on my tongue and it came out, "the Grest," and that concocted word became our favorite compliment to each other. We would write it in notes, birthday cards, Valentine's cards, or any other note or letter to the other. It remained our special compliment over the years.

I followed the doctor into the hallway. A few steps down from the doorway, she stopped and faced me. I started to ask a question, but before I could form a word, I started crying. The doctor looked like she was going to cry, the tears welling in her eyes, but she held it together much better than I did. It took me twenty or thirty seconds to suppress the crying. I didn't want to ask this question. I was terrified of what the answer would be.

"How scared should we be?" I finally blurted out.

The doctor took a deep breath. "It doesn't look good," she said tenderly.

"DAMN!" I screamed inside my head. I started crying again.

That simple statement marked the most pivotal of all our dreadful moments. It was the first time a doctor or medical professional said that she was nearing death in any terms.

"But," the doctor quickly continued, "that is my assessment, and I'm not as familiar with her history and her overall condition. Her oncologist is reviewing her charts now, and she and her team, who know Melanie much better than I do, may have a different outlook."

"How long would you expect her to have left?" I asked, quickly adding, "Should I be calling people in to say goodbye?" I started crying again, but somewhat more contained.

"I would say anywhere from a few weeks to a few months, but again, her primary care team might give her more time than that." The doctor paused then added, "Much of it depends on getting her liver biopsied and determining next steps from there."

The news was horribly grim, but they still had plans. They still had actionable ideas. They were still working the problems. It wasn't immediate. She didn't have only hours or days left. She had a few weeks to a few months, and maybe more.

9

Janis and Bobby

After the doctor gave me the bleak prognosis in the hallway, I walked past Melanie's door and went into the Family Room. I sat down and lost my shit. I cried nonstop for probably about 15 minutes. When I finally regained some composure, I stepped to the windows and again looked out over Forest Park and the pathways of the American Cancer Society's annual Making Strides Walk. This year's walk was a little over seven months away. I stared at the pathways we would follow.

I could see us walking those pathways without her. I could see myself trailing behind a large pack of our friends and family, standing on that pathway staring back up at this window, and Melanie would be gone.

It was real. This wasn't a panicked reaction. This wasn't an irrational, conjured fear. I had been explicitly told this by a doctor, an expert medical professional.

I called Stephanie. I told her what was happening, broken by pauses as I fought to control my crying. It was a lot to process and absorb for her in a short time.

"Can you get the kids and bring them up here?" I asked her after I finished my explanations.

"Wait," she exclaimed. "Are you saying it's time for them to say goodbye to her?"

"No!" I said quickly and emphatically then collected my thoughts. "They aren't telling me it's that urgent, but it's looking like it will be a long weekend, and maybe even several tough days beyond that. They want to biopsy her liver, which is an invasive surgery, as you know, so she'll be out for that and then recovery. The kids might not be able to see her for a few days if we don't get them up here today."

"Okay, okay," Stephanie said. We spoke more about the logistics. I made a few other calls and sent text messages. Megan was already on a plane flying in. I headed back in to see Melanie. She was still sleeping. I watched her chest rise and fall as she steadily drew breaths. Her head was covered with prickly stubble. After missing a few weeks of chemo, her hair was starting to grow back.

I received and sent more text messages. Vivian was coming to the hospital to visit, and I asked her to see if Stephanie needed any help getting the kids up here. Viv was on it. After some miserable quiet time, the nurse came back into the room.

"They're moving her to the ICU," the nurse informed me.

"Why?" I couldn't prevent the panic in my voice, and I didn't care. *Was her condition suddenly worse? Why was the ICU necessary?*

"They can get her stabilized and prepped for surgery better in the ICU," the nurse said gently, obviously detecting the panic. I took a deep breath and contemplated this unexpected move.

"And by surgery, you mean the biopsy, right?"

"Yes," the nurse responded quickly.

As I was realizing I needed to text Vivian and Steph, a thought occurred to me.

"Wait!" I spoke quickly. "How soon are they moving her? Her sister is bringing our kids up to see her. Can they wait to move her until the kids see her, or can they allow the kids to visit her in the ICU?" I had enough medical experience to know that kids and ICU units were mutually exclusive entities.

"I think they want to keep things moving." The nurse considered the situation. "Let me check with the doctor."

The nurse finished her tasks and left. She was back within minutes.

"We're going to go ahead and get her moved, and the doctor will contact the ICU and make sure they allow the kids to visit her down there, but they'll have to keep the visit short."

A few minutes later, the doctor came back in and recapped the decision to move to the ICU and the reasons behind it. I asked a few questions, but the discussion was brief.

"And the kids will be able to see her down there, right? If they aren't going to let them see her, I'd rather we wait here so they can see her. They'll be here soon."

"I already spoke to the head of the unit. They'll allow the kids to see her, but only for a few minutes."

"I understand." I nodded. "As long as they get to see her."

Things moved quickly. I gathered Melanie's things and stuffed them in her bags. They were wheeling her out of the room within minutes, and I was texting updates as we scurried through the hallways. Stephanie was already on the way with the kids, and Vivian was meeting her to help walk them in.

When we got to the ICU, they took Melanie in but asked me to wait in the outer waiting room while they got her settled. The ICU was locked down tight. An ICU nurse came to me in the waiting room to brief me on the ICU ground rules. She rattled off a few procedural things initially.

"And we only allow two visitors back in the room at a time," she informed me.

"Okay, but how do you want to do that with the kids?" I asked. "We have four kids. Do you want to take them back one or two at a time, or get them all back there at once and get it over with?"

"I'm sorry," she said, looking genuinely sorry. "Children are not allowed in the ICU."

"NO!" I exclaimed. "I discussed this with the doctor up in her other room before they moved her, and she said the kids would be allowed to see her. The doctor said she called the head of the unit down here and confirmed it."

"Well," she said doubtfully, "I'll have to check with the head of the unit but…"

"Look," I said, shaking my head, "I understand it isn't your decision, and I don't mean to be an ass to you, but my kids are seeing their mom, and she is seeing her kids. I don't care what the head doctor says. If I have to go get Melanie and wheel her out here to see them, I will, but they are seeing her one way or the other regardless what anybody says."

"Okay." She put her hands up. "But I have to confirm with the head of the unit, my supervisor. Give me a few minutes, okay?"

"I understand," I said as peacefully as I could manage.

She disappeared just as the elevator dinged. I heard the screeching of familiar little voices, which Steph silenced before I rounded the corner. We waited at least 10 or 15 minutes—an eternity when trying to keep little kids quiet and contained. Viv had joined Stephanie, so fortunately, we had a good containment crew. And a vending machine. Snacks help.

"Oh, good. They're all here!" The ICU nurse was back and smiling. "You understand it will need to be a short visit. We'll take them all back together and give them about 10 minutes."

"Works for me," I said.

"And you can help me walk them back," she said.

"Fine with us," I said. "But, can Stephanie help us keep the kids corralled? Then she can walk them out when their visit is over?"

"That sounds good," the nurse answered after mulling it over.

As we moved through the maze of hallways and secure doors, I wondered how any visitors would figure out how to get back here. We could worry about that later. The nurse was walking fast, and I quickened my pace to catch up with her.

"Hey," I said in a conciliatory tone, "I didn't mean to give you a hard time out there before. I know you were stuck in the middle of it all." I knew Melanie would appreciate me making the peace. I'd learned a few things from her.

"Oh, don't worry about it." She brushed the air with her hand. "I have a couple of kids too, and in your situation, I would have been just the same. I hope my husband would too." She smiled. "My supervisor did talk to the other doctor and approved it. He just forgot to tell me." She rolled her eyes.

We were cool. Melanie would have been pleased.

The kids' visit was short. It appeared to me that Melanie had been given some new med, which was making her groggy. The younger kids climbed on her on the bed for a minute, and then they were in the back of the long rectangular-shaped room. Melanie's bed was near the sliding door and curtain in the front, which left ample room behind her bed for a couch that folded out into a bed under the window. The youngest two were jumping on the couch and looking out the window. The older two talked to Melanie for a few minutes, and then the kids were whisked off. Stephanie's husband, Allen, had come up to take the kids home, and then Stephanie stayed back in the room with me for a bit.

We did our best to honor the two-visitor rule. We rotated out so Viv could come in, then when Megan arrived, we continued our rotation. We ended up breaking the rule a couple times as three of us lingered. At one point there were four of us, and a nurse broke up our little party. Viv went home, and then later, so did Steph. Megan and I hung out with Melanie for a few more hours.

They were running tests and monitoring her constantly. Megan volunteered to stay the night, and the attending doctor thought that was a good idea. Before I left for the evening, dialysis was mentioned for the first time. I had only a general idea of what dialysis was or why they would do it. The doctor explained that her liver function had diminished, which I already knew, and then he explained that the liver filters toxins out of the blood and, therefore, out of the body. These toxins were increasing in her bloodstream, and it was affecting her. Dialysis would clean her blood and filter out the toxins, effectively doing the job her liver was supposed to do. When I thought she seemed groggier during the kids' visit, I assumed it was a new medication, but it was actually the effect of these toxins. It made her seem a little drunk.

They decided not to begin dialysis tonight. Instead, they would continue to monitor her and complete other tests. Before I left, the doctor summoned me out into the hallway. He used his pen to point at something on a piece of paper. It was my cell phone number.

"Is this your correct cell phone number?" he asked, and I confirmed. "I need you to be available. Keep the phone by you with the ringer on in case we need to call. Can you do that?"

"Yeah, but—"

"The toxins I explained to you are impairing her thinking and her judgment. If we need to start dialysis or anything else, I'll need to get your approval. You're the designated POA, correct?"

Was that a joke? Was he really asking me that?

We just filled those forms out several hours ago, and we didn't think it was even necessary. I was supposed to take copies home and file them away, in case we needed them years from now. Now, hours later, I was on the verge of exercising those very powers granted in that damn document. The ink from the notary's stamp was barely dry. How did we get here?

"Yeah, I am," I said numbly. Megan came out into the hallway.

"She's asleep," Megan told us.

"Should I stay?" I looked from Megan to the doctor. "I want to be here… If…"

The doctor shook his head. "We aren't there. If her numbers get worse, we can start the dialysis. We'll call you immediately if we reach that point." We discussed the situation for a few more minutes, and the doctor left us.

"Get home, Paddy," Megan said. "Get some rest and take care of those kiddos. I'll be with her. I'll be here all night. Like the doctor said, we'll call you if anything comes up."

"Yeah…"

Generally, duty as a father and duty as a husband go hand in hand. This was one dreadful time when they were at odds.

The kids were already asleep, so I didn't see them when I got home. It was Friday night, so no school tomorrow. I had already arranged with family and friends to cover activities for the next day. I was driving my oldest to take the SAT early in the morning. It was at a location not too far from the hospital, so I could get there earlier than usual.

My phone rang while I was getting dressed that morning. It was Megan and the doctor. I don't remember exactly why they called or what we talked about, only that they called. It wasn't to approve dialysis as I might have expected or to grant permission for anything else. It was only an update on her condition. I think the doctor did strongly suggest that I get there soon. I believe I told him my time frame, which he replied was good. I hung out with the younger ones until their rides arrived, and then the oldest and I hit the road.

I got to the hospital as quickly as possible. No stopping for fountains or anything else this time. I was a little surprised, then relieved, when things seemed about the same as they did last night, although that relief wouldn't last long. Melanie was noticeably groggier, like a drunk who had kept on drinking. She wasn't communicating at all. After talking to Melanie briefly, she closed her eyes and settled back onto her pillow. Megan gave me a look, and we stepped out into the hallway.

"This doctor is an *asshole*!" Megan was fuming but kept her voice hushed. "I am *not* a fan, and neither is Melanie!"

"Well, then I'm not a fan either." I shook my head. I was wondering if we had another Number Two on our hands—Number Two Jr. I didn't bother to ask her why she wasn't a fan because I knew she was going to tell me anyway. She had that look.

"He freaking said to us that dialysis was a Hail Mary!"

Damn.

"He said Hail Mary?"

"Yes! He said 'Hail Mary'—*to Melanie!*"

I sighed. "How did Melanie take that?"

"Oh, she was *pissed!* She was asking him what that meant. She was *not* happy."

"At least he's giving us a straight answer," I said after thinking it over. "If that's what's happening, I'm at least glad to know."

"Whatever," Megan responded. "I mean…what kind of doctor flippantly tells someone in this situation that what they're doing is a Hail Mary? What an *asshole!*"

I tried to think, but I didn't know what to think. I just kept shaking my head.

"Oh! And then he told us he shouldn't have let *us* talk *him* out of starting dialysis last night!"

"What?" I thought about the conversation the previous night. "He didn't say anything about wanting to start dialysis last night."

"*Exactly!* Asshole."

One thing I've learned about people, far more than I ever knew before this experience with Melanie, is how much you see love in anger. With every word I heard Megan say, I felt the love she had for Melanie, and she was hellbent on protecting her.

Besides, Megan was right. I have enormous respect for medical providers, but they're human. They make mistakes and say stupid things like the rest of us. They make up a community of ultra-intelligent individuals with colossal responsibility on their shoulders every day. I can appreciate the coping mechanisms they must develop to do what they do. When I make a mistake or say something stupid on my job, people don't die or have their soul crushed. The medical community bears such burdens. Number Two Jr. seemed like an ass, but I didn't have the energy to worry about him. I just hoped he was good at his job.

I was battle-worn, desperate, and weary. I wasn't inclined to expend a single calorie of my energy on anything besides Melanie. Megan was the high-powered New York attorney who spent her days battling for employees' rights. She was a champion of the oppressed. She loved Melanie dearly, and she was primed to defend her. I was glad to have her on our side. It was like having an attack dog at your side in a bad neighborhood on a dark night. I was cradled in a world of hard-core, badass women, and I liked that. It wasn't threatening to me in any way. I wasn't anticipating any confrontations or issues, but if there were any, I was comfortable enough to let a girl fight a battle or two for me. I was so grateful that Megan was there. If Number Two Jr. or anyone else caused us any grief, I'd hang by Melanie's side and let Megan tear them to shreds. It would probably be fun to watch.

"And then he told her she wasn't clear-minded enough to make her own decisions, and he said it all flippantly like some kind of asshole!" Megan continued.

I sighed.

"He told her that?"

"*Yes!*"

"What did she say?" I asked.

"Oh, she was NOT HAPPY!"

I sighed again and rolled my eyes.

"Then he told her he was going to do everything he could for her because she has four little kids at home."

"*What?*"

"Yeah. He actually said that—*to her!*"

I closed my eyes. *What an asshole.* I tried to put it all out of my head. I wanted to focus on Melanie, not worry about some asshole doctor.

"That was when we called you this morning," she continued.

"Wait." I thought back to the phone call. "Why did he tell her she wasn't thinking clearly enough to make her own decisions? He didn't ask for any decisions when he called. He just gave me an update."

"Because he's an asshole!" Megan explained.

I sighed yet again. We went back in the room to be with Melanie. She was sleeping. We talked quietly about nothing special. I saw Megan glance into the hallway and then back to me with an intense look of disgust right before Number Two Jr. stepped into the room. He asked me to step into the hallway with him.

The conversation was brief but long enough for him to demonstrate why Megan and Melanie had such a strong dislike for him. Dialysis was a necessity for any other treatment on Melanie to be possible. They had to try to filter the toxins out of her bloodstream. I had to give my approval, exercising the power of attorney that yesterday we almost didn't fill out because we thought it wasn't needed. I said yes, and dialysis was immediately ordered.

It took *forever* for the dialysis machine and technician to show up, and then there was a problem with the machine. Megan was fuming, and it grew more tense by the minute. Melanie was fighting for her life against an invasion of fatal toxins in a time-critical battle, but delays and glitches ruled the next couple hours. They finally got it started, and it would take a few hours for the dialysis cycle to complete.

Stephanie showed up with her husband, Allen. We texted updates to others, and other friends showed up. We busted the two-visitor rule, and no one said anything to us. That seemed like a bad sign.

After a couple hours of dialysis, her numbers were not improving. That seemed like a bad sign. After another thirty or forty minutes, the numbers were worse. That wasn't just a bad sign, that was an end sign.

Some medical professional, it may have been the dialysis technician or someone else, informed us that she was now in total liver failure. Dialysis couldn't keep up with the toxins spilling into her bloodstream.

Total liver failure.

Those words sliced through me. You didn't need a medical degree to feel the impact of those words.

For another hour or so, the dialysis process continued, but her numbers only continued to worsen. They asked me if I wanted to stop dialysis. I don't remember how they phrased it, but they were essentially asking me if I wanted to accept the inevitable or let the process run its course. We don't stop fighting. I refused to stop anything. Miracles only happen when you don't stop fighting. Number Two Jr. appeared and once again summoned me into the hallway. He explained the situation, but it wasn't anything I didn't already know.

"I need to be certain that you understand what is happening," he said in a way that annoyed me, but maybe I was primed to be annoyed by him.

"I understand, but I'm waiting for you to pull a miracle out of your hat," I responded flatly.

"No, I need to know that you know what is about to happen," he repeated. He seemed to be making a concerted effort to maximize the condescension.

"I understand," I replied, looking him straight in the eye. "I'm not delusional. I know what is happening. But I need to be certain that you understand that we don't stop fighting—ever. We won't stop fighting until the fight is taken from us." I could see Melanie through a gap in the curtain from where we were standing. I looked briefly at her. She was curled up in bed in a fetal position. I looked him back in the eye. "That's how we roll in our family. So, you just go work on a miracle for us—you know, since she has four kids and all. I'll be right here with her."

He said nothing. I don't think he expected an answer like that. I saw the blank stare of the doofus betray the facade of the alpha. I had no more use for him, so I turned away and went back into the room. I never saw him again.

Melanie was getting restless. She was confused and in a strange daze. She would lay back in bed, babbling incoherently. Then, suddenly, she would prop up in bed as if she would leap out of it. She would be exclaiming gibberish, as if she were scared of something. Within a few minutes, a nurse summoned me out into the hallway.

"If you would like, we could administer something to make her comfortable."

I knew that "Make her comfortable" meant give her a painkiller that would settle her down and make her peaceful—knock her unconscious, in other words. The nurse never said, "Until she dies." She didn't need to say it. Once again, I executed the power of attorney that, less than 20 hours earlier, I was certain we didn't need. I didn't want to give up the fight, but I didn't want to make her suffer out of delusional ignorance. "Make her comfortable" was the perfect notion, and I wanted her as comfortable as possible, suffering as little as possible. I said yes to that.

They were out of actionable ideas. They had no plans. There were no more tests. Treatment was over. Now, the only thing to do was "make her comfortable" and wait it out, but I refused to stop hoping for a miracle even though I understood the inevitability.

Our clan was texting and making calls ceaselessly. I let the others handle most of that as I succumbed to the numbness. Then my phone rang in my pocket. It hadn't rung much in days. It was cousin David, the rock of our cancer journey. I stepped back out in the hallway to speak with him. He asked what was happening, and I explained the best I could.

"I'm so sorry, Paddy. That sucks," he said when I finished updating him.

That was when I fully accepted the course of action being taken. His was the confirmation I needed in order to deal with the inescapable. For years, with every significant development in Melanie's condition, we would speak with David. He would listen to what was happening, at times even making calls and contacting doctors he knew to confirm diagnosis and treatments. He consistently did this in a positive manner that reassured us and gave us hope. He and his wife, Beth, also a doctor, were rocks for us. Whenever we spoke to them, I always came away feeling like we were on the best possible course, fighting and winning.

When David had nothing to offer about tests, treatments, plans, or actionable ideas, it confirmed that the course we were on was the only course we could be on, as much as it hurt. When David had nothing more to say, it gave me confidence that Number Two Jr. and the rest of the medical staff were doing all they could.

When I went back into the room, several more friends and family members had arrived, but there was a telling absence of medical staff. When nurses did come by, they said nothing to us about the two-visitor rule, which we had shattered. Texts and calls were feverishly being sent and received, and more friends and family continued to arrive. Melanie was sedated, lying still and quiet on her side. Stephanie climbed into bed with her only sister and spooned her, cuddling, snuggling, and whispering gently in her ear.

The eerie similarity of my dad's final hours added to my dread. When my dad lost consciousness, we spent a few hours watching his vital signs decline and his breathing slow until finally his breathing ceased and his vital signs disappeared. When I first noticed a decline in Melanie's vital signs, someone asked a nurse point-blank how long Melanie had left. The nurse said everyone was different, and there was no way to tell. She said it could be a few hours to a few days, but I couldn't shake the feeling that it would go the same way as my previous experience.

Melanie couldn't have been surrounded by a more perfect group of friends and family. There was at least a dozen of us. Over the next few hours, we cried and talked in waves. Someone would cry, which would overpower the rest of us, and we would all cry together and hug one another. The crying would subside, and we would tell stories about Melanie and our lives together, even laughing at times about our antics. We took turns sitting at Melanie's side and talking to her. It was horrendous and devastating yet marvelous and comforting at the same time.

And then there was Janis.

I always considered Melanie crazy in all the right ways. She didn't need to be the center of attention, but she wasn't afraid to be in the spotlight. We had a group of friends that liked to get out and have fun—barhopping, seeing bands, going to the wild Mardi Gras festivities in St. Louis every year, and any other good night out. On multiple occasions over the years, Melanie had gotten up on stage with one of the local bands and sang Janis Joplin's "Me and Bobby McGee." The most memorable performance of that was on our wedding night.

Our wedding reception was in a hall on Laclede's Landing in downtown St. Louis. After our reception, we went over to the Trainwreck Saloon, a three-story bar and restaurant also on the Landing. The bottom floor had a stage where bands performed. Melanie and I met in front of that stage through our mutual friend Claire, who I like to refer to as The Reason since Claire was the reason we met.

On our wedding night, I stood next to The Reason in front of that stage. Melanie got on stage with the band, in her wedding dress, and sang Janis's "Me and Bobby McGee" while being cheered on by friends and family.

Many of those same friends and family were now gathered around Melanie's bed. Crutcher, our great friend, cued up "Me and Bobby McGee" on her phone and set it on the bed next to Melanie and let it play.

Within a few hours, just after 6:00 P.M., Melanie's vital signs were declining rapidly. I didn't realize it was possible for blood pressure to drop so low and yet still have blood pressure. At one point, I looked at the monitor and it read something like 37 over 24. Her breathing was becoming shallower and slowing in cadence. The time between breaths increased, while her body would lay distressingly motionless.

I screamed an F-bomb at the side of her bed. I thought she'd appreciate that. It seemed appropriate, and I couldn't have stopped it if I tried. I owed her that one.

I watched her chest barely rise and fall after an unsettling duration. I was at her side with my hand on her head; the stubbly hairs felt both prickly and fuzzy. Stephanie was on the other side of her, holding her hand. For at least 20 seconds, and maybe longer, she was perfectly still. Then, her mouth opened slightly, her chest heaved, and she quickly gulped in another breath.

"Suck it, Trebek," I mumbled as I touched my forehead to her head, my mouth close to her ear. I was so proud of her.

She was still fighting.

This hard-core, badass, tough-as-nails warrior wouldn't let go.

"You're the Grest!" I whispered in her ear. "I love you so much. I'm so proud of you."

And then, after another long interval, she did it again. She drew another breath.

And then another.

She wouldn't give up. She wouldn't stop fighting. She never stopped fighting. Finally, the fight was taken away from her—from us.

I cried uncontrollably. When I looked up, the nurse was standing at the side of the bed. She had her hands folded in front of her, and she stood there doing nothing.

"The doctor is on the way in." She didn't say why. She didn't need to.

I don't recall the doctor coming in and pronouncing, but I was aware it happened. It wasn't Number Two Jr. I do remember that. The nurse removed the last of the wires and tubes. There were no more beeps or buzzes or dings or hisses or hums. The only sounds that remained were of our friends and family crying and consoling one another.

I was summoned into the hallway to sign some forms. I believe I was granting permission to release the body, or something of that nature, and there was information from Mid America Transplant. Melanie had donated her eyes. I had forgotten that she had done that, although I recalled her telling me long ago. About a month later,

I'd receive a letter that Melanie's eyes had restored the vision of two people. What a gift. It just seemed so Melanie. I was in awe of the fact that two people now got to see the world, literally and figuratively, through Melanie's eyes.

We loitered in the room and the hallway for probably an hour. I couldn't make sense of it. My mind wavered between understanding and disbelief. She was gone, and I knew it. It isn't that hard to understand death, yet it didn't make any sense that she was gone. Death was incomprehensible. How could her body be right there in front of me yet lifeless? I was in the middle of something that I didn't understand, which seemed to be a recurring theme of my life, but never quite like this.

Where did she go?

She hadn't gone anywhere. She was right there.

That wasn't her.

Then what was that?

I understood perfectly.

I didn't understand anything.

"Now comes the hardest part," Crutcher said to me.

"What's that?" I asked. Crutcher was devastatingly experienced in such events. Her son and daughter had been born prematurely, and her daughter passed when she was about a year old. Within a matter of years, she would lose her dad and then her brother, who unexpectedly died from a brain aneurism. Crutcher had unenviable credibility in this situation.

"Leaving," Crutcher said flatly. "It's so hard to walk away."

We hugged. My reaction was that it wouldn't be that hard to walk away. We'd been dealing with this for so long, processing the finality for hours now. She had passed, so why hang around with her lifeless body? That seemed morbid. While Crutcher's caveat didn't feel applicable to me, it burrowed into my mind.

Stephanie came up to me minutes later. "Do you think she knew she was dying?" she asked me, distressed by her own question.

"What does it matter?" I replied, and then I instantly felt bad for responding as I did. "I don't mean that, like…like I'm mad you asked. I've been thinking the same thing, but then I keep wondering why I care or why it matters. I don't know. Does it matter?"

Stephanie stared blankly for a few moments. I was feeling sick that I'd somehow upset her—beyond what she already was.

"You're right!" she softly exclaimed. "It doesn't matter. You're so right." She said these words slowly and deliberately, as if she'd had a great revelation, which conversely helped me somewhat reconcile this question for myself. There were plenty of other questions and thoughts and emotions to process, and they kept pounding on my mind and body.

The strange thing was, I didn't understand why it did or didn't matter. It was just a feeling, and it was among many things that I didn't want to think about or feel.

One of our friends came over to me in the hallway. "You know, Melanie told me she never questioned or doubted her care until these blood clots started happening in her leg."

I don't remember which friend it was. I think I can't specifically remember who it was because I had this same conversation three or four times over that hour, and each instance blends in my memory so that I can't distinguish them. In the days and weeks to follow, I had essentially this same conversation several more times with other friends.

I nodded. I knew the intention behind this conversation because I'd repeatedly thought the same thing. Melanie and I discussed it multiple times. It wasn't that anyone was suggesting lawsuits. I think we were all just trying to make sense of what happened; there were so many things to make sense of. After we learned that blood clots could be common in cancer patients, we were never clear if it was related directly to the cancer itself or the chemo, the drugs, or a combination of all of the above, but multiple medical professionals had told us it was not uncommon.

Like Melanie, I had never questioned or doubted her care, especially since David always validated her treatment when we had questions. When we learned later how common blood clots were in cancer patients, we wondered why they hadn't done tests and taken action when she started having leg pain weeks earlier. Her leg pain had preceded even her initial vision stroke by days, but they didn't do any tests or suggest treatment when she complained about it. If it was so common, we wondered why they didn't recognize that and do something—anything. If they had recognized the possibility, could they have caught it sooner, prevented the strokes, and treated her liver before her condition worsened? I was learning that Melanie and I weren't the only ones who wondered about this.

"I know." I nodded. "Believe me, we've been wondering that for weeks, but I really don't think it would have mattered. Cancer affects everyone differently, but hers was incredibly aggressive. Even when she initially went through chemo, and with three different chemo drugs, radiation, and a double mastectomy, and everything else, it still metastasized. It still spread into her bones. It kept spreading even with chemo pills and when she resumed full chemo treatments. I think if it hadn't been for the treatments and care she received, it would have killed her two or three years ago. I think they gave us two or three more years with her than we would've had. I'm grateful for that. Maybe they could've given her a few more weeks, but this shit has been spreading and attacking her for years. Cancer just sucks. There's only so much they can do. It just sucks."

Each time I had this conversation, the person I said these things to would simply nod and seem to agree and accept the inevitability of it all. What else was there to do?

We continued loitering in the hallway, drifting back in and out of the room. No one was leaving. No one seemed to want to leave. I went back in the room and put my hand on Melanie's cheek. My entire body jerked when I did. It stunned me how cold she had gotten and how fast. It felt like touching a cold marble block, and the sensation was in total agreement with the conclusion that my mind still insisted on rejecting.

I was back out in the hallway, drifting from loved one to loved one, giving and receiving hugs. I don't remember how or why the next thought came to mind. I don't know if someone mentioned something or if I just thought of it, but it was a devastating thought.

The kids.

How do you go home and tell four young children that their mother had died?

How do I tell four kids, who I love dearly and want to protect from anything bad, that their MOM is DEAD?

What would I say to them?

How do I do that?

I felt like I might fall to my knees.

I wanted to throw up.

At the first indication that it might be time to leave, I was overwhelmed by Crutcher's caveat about how hard it would be. I didn't know how to leave. I felt powerless and incapable of walking away.

How could I leave Melanie there? That would make it real. Was it real? What if she wasn't really gone? We shouldn't leave her alone. What if she woke up after we left? What if the doctors were wrong? How could I leave her and never see her or talk to her again? That feeling exponentially amplified the dreadful and distressing apprehension that I had to tell our kids that mom was gone.

I don't remember walking away. I don't remember walking out of the hospital at all. My sister, Liz, insisted on driving me home, which was likely an excellent idea. Her husband, Brian, drove our car home for me. We decided to get dinner, a good idea since I probably hadn't had half a meal in two days. It was late, and the kids would already be in bed. It would be better to let them get a good night's sleep and tell them in the morning. We'd spend the day tomorrow dealing with it rather than keeping them up all night.

As we drove away from the hospital, we turned onto Kingshighway Boulevard, which ran alongside Forest Park. I peered into the darkness of the massive park and thought again about the American Cancer Society's Making Strides Walk. My fear that we would be walking the walk without Melanie this year, and every year to come, was now a reality, an unreal reality.

My new reality.

Our new reality.

When I got home, the kids were asleep. Whenever I think about this, it always seems poetically appropriate that the person who watched our kids on the night Melanie died was a Camp Kesem counselor. She was a graduate with whom Melanie had established a strong relationship, and she would remain a dear family friend—and she wasn't the only CK counselor that happened with. Since most of the people I might have called to watch the kids that night had been at the hospital, I called on some trusted CK love. I gave her the news, and we talked for a bit before she left. The long night continued.

I didn't sleep that night. I have had plenty of nights I would call sleepless nights. I had many such nights in the few preceding weeks. I never had a night like that before. Usually, I would get drowsy and doze off a few times. Not that night. No dozing off. No waking up with confusion. No trying to sort out lost time.

I was alert, vividly awake the entire night. I walked around the house, pacing back and forth. I sat at the kitchen table. I sat on the edge of the bed. I sat on the sofa. In my mind, I told each of my kids, hundreds of times, that their mom had passed away. I considered and practiced what I would say to each one, carefully choosing age-appropriate words and statements, forming scripts in my mind.

When I realized the curtains were starting to glow, illuminated by the morning sun, and the details of the room came into focus, my stomach churned with dread. How could I do this? I remember hearing the scraping sound of one of the bedroom doors opening, and then I barely remember a single detail. The kids came out one by one. I sat with each of them. The smaller ones on my lap. I have no idea what exactly I said to any of them. The hours of practicing over the entire night were lost, and I spoke from the heart to each of them.

I do remember how amazingly well they took the news. They were mostly quiet but asked some questions. We hugged and cuddled and snuggled. They were so strong. They were gracious and accommodating to one another, especially as each child woke and came out to receive the news. It was a prelude to the weeks and months to come. They were exuding Melanie's spirit, continuing to display and project kindness and compassion even as they were suffering their own tragedy. I was in awe of them.

On Monday, the kids went back to school, and they continued to handle everything with strength and admirable resiliency. Like their mom, they kept bringing joy to everything they did. From there, life just kept moving along. Time and life stop for nothing. Kids still need to eat, groceries still need to be bought, laundry still needs to be done, trash has to be taken out, dishes still need to be cleaned, and so on and so forth.

With a little help from my friends, funeral planning began on Monday. Vivian and Tiffani, our amazing friends who had spent countless hours with Melanie during treatment and hospital stays and who were part of the clan in the ICU at the end, accompanied me on multiple trips to the funeral offices and cemetery. They helped pick out Melanie's casket, which was a super fun job. They wrote her obituary, and they handled numerous other surreal and morbid tasks in preparation for the funeral.

On Tuesday, I packed lunches, got kids dressed, and sent them off to school again. I was numb. I started a load of laundry, a load of dirty towels. I checked emails. I emptied the dishwasher. I put the clean dishes away. I loaded the dirty dishes into the now-empty dishwasher. I went down and switched the laundry. I put the towels in the dryer. Life just kept moving along. If someone who didn't know me had observed me, it would have looked like an ordinary ho-hum day. I remained numb.

I took a shower and changed clothes. I sat on the edge of the bed and pulled my socks on, and then I sat there thinking about Melanie and our life together. When I thought about The Escape Clause Revelation, a brief flurry of strong and conflicting emotions prodded the numbness but couldn't penetrate it. It was as if I'd lost the ability to feel anything. I was sitting in the same spot on the edge of the bed where I'd been sitting when that revelation had struck.

I went back downstairs to switch laundry, putting the freshly dried towels into an empty laundry basket. As I walked to the staircase, I thought about the night Melanie met me on the stairs. As I carried the basket of towels up, I thought about how I'd carried her up the stairs that night. As I walked past the kitchen table, I thought about the Christopher Walken comment and the subsequent revival of giddy fun we shared that evening. I scanned the pictures of her with friends and family that covered the table, waiting to become collages for the funeral.

As I looked at the multitude of loved ones in the pictures, I thought about Melanie as the Yoda of friendship. The Jedi Master of relationships. Despite all these memories assailing me with every step, I didn't react emotionally. I felt too empty inside, void, numb. My world was bleak, dismal, and desolate.

I dropped the laundry basket onto the floor in the living room in front of the sofa. I grabbed a solid blue towel and tossed it into the air. I caught it in the middle and let each side drape down on opposite sides of my hands to make the first fold, then folded it more and tossed the folded square onto the ottoman to start a stack.

I grabbed the next towel. It was one of the kids' towels, a Star Wars towel. I saw the faces of young Anakin and young Obi-Wan as I snatched up the extra-long beach towel. Due to the length, I tossed it up in the air over my head higher than the first. When I caught it and the sides draped down around my hands, the bottom of the towel flared out before me and revealed a large image of Yoda standing with a look of intense determination on his face. He loomed over me, staring into my eyes, his arm outstretched and his hand raised, an image that was supposed to convey using the Force in some way. It also appeared like a priest or pastor raising his hand to bestow a blessing. Only moments earlier, I was reflecting on how I thought of Melanie as my Yoda, the Jedi Master of relationships, and now suddenly Yoda was looming over me, extending his hand in a blessing and staring intently into my eyes.

As Melanie would say, I lost my shit.

I let out some horrific bellowing, wailing sound. It could have been a noise Chewbacca might make, but far more hideous. I collapsed to the floor. I've seen things like this in movies and television shows where someone totally loses control, but it always seemed melodramatic and fake to me. I didn't think I'd ever really lose my shit that bad for any reason, but it was involuntary and real. My knees buckled, and I collapsed helplessly.

I fell into a heap on the floor, crying and wailing uncontrollably for several minutes. I'd never cried that hard in my life. I didn't cry that hard when she died. It was an entirely new tier of pain. My eyes burned fiercely. My head felt like it was being split open.

But those were just the physical pains.

I'd learned a deeper love when the fear had set in after The Escape Clause Revelation, but now I discovered an even deeper level when the pain took hold.

And then I lost time—literally.

I looked around completely disoriented, unable to determine where I was momentarily. I had somehow moved without being aware of doing it. The last thing I was consciously aware of was being huddled on the floor wailing. The next thing I was aware of was sitting up with my back against the sofa. When I looked around the room, it seemed wrong and unfamiliar because it wasn't the point of view I should have been seeing, and it took me a while to realize exactly where I was and recognize my own living room. I was now sitting against the exact spot of the sofa where Melanie had been sitting when I rushed home from the grocery store while she was in the throes of the speech stroke. My butt was pressed into the floor in the exact spot where her feet were when I pulled the acceptable pants up over her hips seconds before the responders walked in. I had no recollection of moving myself into this spot.

I sat there crying in waves for a few minutes. Sometimes a wave of intense bellowing would overtake me, and then it would subside into sobbing until the next wave gripped me. When I finally felt as if the waves were subsiding entirely, I realized I was still holding the towel. I held it out and looked at Yoda again, losing my shit all over again. I bellowed again as I twisted the towel in my hands. I squeezed intensely as if I were trying to wring that little green Muppetf***er right out of the towel, as if I could somehow squeeze him out to bring Melanie back. I threw the towel over my head and let it drape over me, sobbing within it.

After several minutes, I recovered, at least as much as you can recover three days after your best friend and partner dies. I went back to folding towels until my phone rang. I looked at the caller ID. It was Steve, our pastor.

"Hey," I answered.

"Hey, buddy," Steve responded, in a typically relaxed manner. That's what I liked about Steve. He wasn't pious or preachy. It was a major factor in how we became members of our church. When it comes to matters of faith and devotion, I can't stand all that pious and preachy shit. Steve was a regular guy. He was a sports fan. We played fantasy football together, drinking beer at our annual draft.

He had an immense faith, but he acted like a guy from my college basketball team. "How you holding up?" he asked.

There was a long pause as I thought about that. "I don't know," I bluntly replied. "I meeean…this sucks."

"Yeah," Steve said, "I can't imagine." He paused. "But you hold it together so well. You always maintain that even keel. You never seem like anything bothers you."

"Oh, I don't know," I responded. "I have my moments. You should have been here about fifteen minutes ago."

"Oh? Why's that?" Steve asked. "You okay?"

"Eh, I'm fine," I responded. I didn't really know how to explain to my pastor that I was trying to wring a little green Muppetf***er out of a towel, so I moved on. "So, what's up?"

"We need to go over the program for the funeral service," Steve said. "But we can do this later if this is a bad time."

"No, it's fine," I said. "Let's get 'er done."

Steve began going over the sequence of events that would comprise the church service. I always got confused on what to call that. I grew up Catholic, although I'd given up Catholicism for Lent years earlier, which sounds like a joke but is actually how it happened. In Catholicism, church services are called "mass," so saying "service" always seemed so generic to me. Was that a worship time like mass, or was it service like getting the oil changed on your car? I could never stand all the religious mumbo jumbo. I just cared about God.

I don't remember who came up with the idea first, but there was a particular song that a friend of ours, a member of the church, sang beautifully. We wanted that in the "service." After a few more procedural points, Steve hit on something I had not thought about yet.

"Have you thought about who you want to do the eulogy?" Steve asked.

It hit me—the importance of that. The eulogy was paramount.

I instantly realized there was no other choice. Melanie deserved to be honored properly in a positive spirit, and no one knew her better than me. Not only did she need to be honored, but I realized it was crucial to set a tone in the spirit of Melanie. We needed this for our kids, our family, our friends, and community. We weren't going to wallow in misery and self-pity. I couldn't trust someone else with this pivotal moment and risk someone botching this. I had to buck up.

It was time to set The Tone. She wouldn't want someone making some sad speech and making everyone miserable. I didn't want that either, and I wouldn't let it happen. This was a woman who turned chemotherapy into a party. This was a woman who befriended a bill collector. This was a woman who lifted up others while in a stare-down with death. I owed her this. She was the most extraordinary person I had ever met. She'd want this tone set for our kids, and she deserved to be honored in a spirit akin to her own spirit.

"If you don't have a family member or friend," Steve said as I mulled it over, "we have people who do this that we can hire. It's not terribly expensive. You give them notes about what you want said about—"

"Oh, hell no!" I cut him off. "I'm doing it."

"You think you can handle that?" Steve asked. "That's going to be tough. This is pretty emotional."

I had experience in public speaking, but this one was obviously far different than any other speaking engagement I'd ever had. Although I wanted to do it, I doubted I could get through it without losing my shit and crying hysterically. I mean, Yoda's image on a towel made me cry alone in my own living room. How could I stand up in front of hundreds of people at her funeral and talk about her? I considered all that. He was right. It would be hard. It didn't matter. It wasn't an option.

Final decision.

10

The Tone of the Extraordinary

The rest of the week was surreal. Everything was muted, blurred, distorted, scrambled, and hazy. It was a week that would never end, and then suddenly it was Friday. Somehow, I had a suit on and was showing up at the church for her wake, and I barely comprehended how I'd gotten there, like I was living in a Kurt Vonnegut novel and had randomly teleported to another time and place.

The funeral director had a couple procedural questions. Stephanie and I monitored the children and tried to pretend we were actual adults who could handle all this. There was a fellowship hall downstairs, which was basically a large cafeteria-style room with a kitchen in the back. I meandered down there and found a crew of friends working diligently to provide food and drinks for everyone. They were hustling and bustling around, and the resulting display revealed their monumental effort.

This scene was a perfect example of the type of thing I wouldn't have appreciated as a younger man but now struck me with a sense of deep appreciation and extensive gratitude. This was just the tip of the iceberg. The way our community had come together for us was nearly as humbling and awe-inspiring as Melanie and her spirit.

I drifted back upstairs. People were starting to arrive. The kids were off with cousins and aunts and uncles. I spoke to people in the hallway outside the back of the sanctuary, and then went in and headed toward the alter—with Melanie in her casket before it. I barely recognized her. Her skin appeared grayish and her face sunken. She looked almost nothing like the young lady I dated and married, and she only slightly resembled the diminished woman I watched deteriorate over the past few months. It was difficult to comprehend that this could be her, and even more perplexing to grasp that this was really happening.

I said a few things to her, struggling to make sense of what I was seeing, and then the funeral director interrupted me. I was inclined to be angry that he insensitively disrupted me while I was having a moment with my wife, but then I was relieved to be wedged away from that tormenting engagement. I answered whatever questions he had and then wandered without definitive purpose to the back of the sanctuary. When I came alongside the back pew, someone stopped me and gave his condolences, and by the time we finished speaking, someone else was waiting behind him to speak with me. By the time I finished speaking with her, there were two or three more parties assembled in formation.

Damn!

I suddenly realized I had found myself in The Line.

Melanie didn't have many directives for her final arrangements. She didn't want to be buried in a wall. You might call that a mausoleum, but in her vernacular, she'd say, "Don't put me in a wall." One required directive she did have was that she didn't want The Line, which she saw as the miserable tradition of a surviving loved one standing next to the coffin of their deceased love so a lineup of people could take turns saying miserably sad things. She thought that was ridiculous and horrible, and she made it unequivocally clear to me myriad times that I should not do The Line at her funeral. Before I realized what was happening, I had allowed myself to fall into precisely the circumstance that Melanie implored me not to permit.

"She was the one person I could talk to about all the crazy stuff at work," one of Melanie's old teaching colleagues, a dear friend Melanie loved, said to me. Melanie had been an elementary school teacher for years until going part-time in recent years to run the library and computer lab. As her cancer battle progressed, she had to quit entirely. "And we stayed in close touch and we'd still talk all the time on the phone about all the madness at work. She was my closest work friend. Who am I gonna talk to about all that crap now?"

I smiled and we hugged. Melanie loved her, and I always enjoyed her company when I saw her at work parties and such. As much as I could have wanted things focused on me as the one who suffered the biggest loss, along with our four kids who just lost their mother, that wasn't my outlook. I appreciated hearing people's feelings about her, and I understood that they lost someone they loved too. We weren't competing over who lost the most. We were sharing our grief and our love for this extraordinary human being.

What I couldn't stand was being pitied. I didn't want anyone feeling sorry for me or the kids. That tone had to be set, and I was determined to make that happen.

"Oh, Paddy," another good friend of Melanie's said to me, "I'm so sorry. This is just so—"

"Thanks," I cut her off. I did it politely, but I wasn't going to tolerate any form of negativity, even if in grief and sadness it could be justified. It wasn't what she was saying, it was how she was saying it. Her tone was not The Tone, and other tones had no place in our lives. It had no place in the spirit of Melanie, a woman who lifted up others even in her darkest moments. I was putting into practice what she had taught me.

"This wasn't a tragedy," I said with a smile. "The only tragedy would have been if we'd never had the chance to get to know her and be her friend. It would have been a tragedy if I didn't get to share my life with her these last couple decades. I've been blessed and I'll continue to be blessed. We all are. Her spirit will always be in us."

"You're so right," the friend said. We hugged and spoke a little more, and then the next party in The Line stepped up.

"She was the best friend I had…" this one began.

"She was the one person I could talk to…" another started.

And then, there was The Rock, cousin David, and his wife Beth, also a doctor and a rock for us.

"I'm sorry, Paddy. It just sucks." After all our cancer consultations, seeing David and Beth at the services closed a circle. His statement made me smile. We once talked about things people say to each other in times of mourning. We all agreed that there were no magic words, and the worst thing to do was to say too much. We concluded that the best thing was to say, "It sucks," and move on. That simple statement was one of the most consoling things I heard that evening. We talked briefly, but The Line was prohibitive.

"Melanie was the one I always talked to…" another person told me.

"She was the only one who understood…" the next one shared.

"What happened to Megan?" Vivian stepped over and asked me.

"One of the kids jumped on her and she wrenched her back," I informed her. With her long dark hair, Megan reminded me of Esmerelda from *The Hunchback of Notre Dame*, and the comparison applied beyond the physical. Esmerelda had a strong sense of justice, standing up to authority and fighting for the mistreated. Megan was an employment law attorney, dedicated to fighting harassment and discrimination in the workplace. Hunched over at Melanie's funeral, I was amused by the irony that she now mimicked Quasimodo.

After several more minutes, Tiffani eased between parties in The Line and brought me a bottle of water. She had a funny smile on her face. "You realize you've got The Line going here, don't you?"

"*I know!*" I exclaimed in a hushed voice. "It just happened. I didn't mean to let a line form. It just did! But now, I can't be rude and walk away from all these people lined up to talk to me. I mean, you know Melanie hated rudeness, so I think that would be worse than The Line."

"I think you're right!" Tiffani laughed lightly. "Besides, it isn't just you." Tiffani pointed toward the front of the sanctuary, which was behind me as I was facing the back. I turned and saw Stephanie, Melanie's lone sibling and the only other immediate family member at the services, standing off to the side of the alter in front of the pews. Their dad, Daun, had his own serious health issues and was on hospice care. I didn't know if he was planning to show up today or tomorrow or what time. Stephanie also now had her own line formed down the side aisle. Her line stretched halfway back along the outer wall and was continuing to grow longer.

"Great," I turned back to face Tiffani. "So now we have *two* lines!"

"Good job, Paddy." Tiffani smiled and drifted away to mingle with other mourners. I turned back to my instance of The Line.

"She was my closest friend..."

"She was the one person I could talk to about all my crazy boyfriend trouble..."

"She was the one person I'd talk to about my kids and family stuff..."

"I can't believe those Kesem counselors!" someone said to me. "There are a bunch of them down in the fellowship hall with your kids. They are just *amazing* with the kids!"

Packs of the Kesem counselors showed up in droves. There had to be dozens of them in the building. I could see them passing by the doors out in the hallway, but none of them had made it to me in The Line yet. It reinforced for me one of those great lessons in life: take advantage of the resources at your disposal. As the night went on, several more people would tell me how awesome they were with the kids down there. It certainly made me feel better. I would have been totally comfortable that my kids were in good hands with all my family and friends around, but those Camp Kesem counselors bring a special magic with them everywhere they go. It didn't surprise me to hear these comments, although I never did find out exactly what they were doing down there that had so many people in such awe of them. Were they consoling the kids? Were they singing songs? Were they playing games? I'd just nod when people would rave about them. It didn't surprise me. Awesome and amazing is what they do.

"Hey," Crutcher came up to me in The Line, "do you remember when you told me in the hospital that there must be twenty or more people who would say Melanie was their best friend?"

I nodded. I remembered saying that to her, and I'd thought it many times.

"You were right, except it is *way* more than that. I must have heard fifty people tonight tell me she was their best friend or the one person they could talk to or something like that."

"I *know*!" I said. "I keep hearing those same comments, like, from every third person who comes up to me."

"How the hell did she even have time to keep up with so many people?" Crutcher asked. It seemed rhetorical, but that didn't stop me from commenting in response.

"I have no idea." I shook my head. "I mean, she was on the phone a lot, but it just doesn't seem possible."

"She was *freaking* amazing," Crutcher said, and I nodded in agreement. "Hey," Crutcher said after a few moments, "I thought you weren't supposed to have a line?"

I threw my arms up in the air. "It just happened! I couldn't stop it!"

We ended up going well past the designated end time of the services. Several uninterrupted hours of interactions and condolences went by with what easily had to be over a thousand people. But it wasn't just the raw numbers that struck me; it was the depth of emotion and sincerity of grief I witnessed. I wondered if it was just me, the biased husband, seeing this, but it wasn't. Numerous others would comment on how amazing it was that Melanie had touched so many people so deeply. At most funerals I've ever attended, usually a significant percentage of people paying their respects don't appear to be experiencing much sense of loss. That was not the experience of Melanie's services. The genuine pain and sadness we witnessed showed what an extraordinary friend she was to so many.

When the last of The Line drifted away, I wanted to sit down for a minute. I'd been standing and talking for several hours, and my entire body had stiffened up. My back was aching. I hadn't taken my first step toward the nearest pew when someone stepped up to me. I don't remember who it was.

"Can you believe that about Daun?"

"What about him?" I realized I had not seen him all night, but that didn't surprise me considering his condition.

"You didn't hear? He passed away this afternoon."

"You've got to be kidding." I immediately looked for Stephanie and headed right for her. Just a few months earlier, she lost her best friend, whom she met as a young girl and had remained friends their entire lives. Now, while mourning at her sister's funeral, she learned her dad died hours earlier.

I don't remember what we said to each other. We hugged. She was wiped out, beyond exhausted, beyond fatigued. She just wanted to get home. Even though she was clearly drained, her typical strength and composure were impressive, as I would observe so many more times in the coming months.

I was so exhausted that I fell asleep quickly after getting the kids to bed, but it wouldn't last. I woke up in the middle of the night. My mind was racing. I sat in the darkness on the edge of the bed. Everything seemed so distant and lonely, like I'd been hovering in isolation endlessly. But before I knew it, I was back in the church, surrounded by family and friends. Everything seemed to drag, yet everything flew by.

I found myself sitting in the front pew with our kids, their mom in a coffin a few feet in front of us. I didn't want them to be there. They had to be there. I didn't want to make them watch their mother's funeral. I didn't want them staring at her lifeless body in a coffin. I didn't want anyone staring at her lifeless body in a coffin, yet here we were.

The service was beautiful, and I tried to shut it all out. I didn't want to hear what was being said, but of course, I heard every word. Not only was this entire experience miserable, I was trying to keep my mind clear of anything emotional so I could get through her eulogy without a complete breakdown. The kids were squirming incessantly, and I welcomed it. I focused on them, trying to filter out the words and images all around me.

And then came the song. A good friend from our church was an astoundingly gifted singer. Melanie had heard her sing the song "Hallelujah" and was so struck by it that Melanie got her to record it. Melanie loved listening to her sing that song, so we asked her to sing it at the service. What I didn't realize, until someone told me later, was that the song has some inappropriate lyrics, but she had rewritten it to something appropriate and sang her modified version. In retrospect, I wish I'd had the foresight to tell them to have her sing it *after* I did the eulogy. Her stunningly beautiful rendition of "Hallelujah" reverberated through my soul, and I feared I would be bawling hysterically before I had a chance to start speaking. I tried not to listen, but that was like trying to ignore the voice of God resonating through your soul. I held it together, but I really don't know how.

I stepped up to the pulpit. I took a deep breath, tried to stop thinking momentarily to clear my head, and then looked to my notes. I didn't have what I was going to say written out. I wasn't going to read from a script. Instead, I had simple talking points to stay on track. I barely looked at those once I got rolling. I wanted to speak from the heart, letting the words come out however they flowed.

I talked about how much fun it was to be with Melanie from the moment we met, quickly realizing I'd never met anyone like her. I explained The Revelation of O'B Clark's. I talked about her friends, my business, and our financial problems. I shared how she befriended the bill collector and turned chemo into a party, lifting others constantly. I told them how she connected with an old college friend at the American Cancer Society and became one of their Portraits of Hope, giving back at the first opportunity.

I'd catch myself starting to cry a few times as I talked, but I'd pause and collect myself and continue on.

I progressed into talking about the strokes, how she could still drop an F-bomb when she couldn't speak otherwise, played match-maker to the doctors, and put her roommate on a pedestal when she could have been focusing on herself in the darkest of her own hours. I don't think I explained that extraordinary moment with Sylvia well enough, inadequately conveying the astounding selflessness and genuine caring for another person, a stranger to her, while she was facing her own death.

Melanie was truly special and unfortunately rare, and I did my best to honor her on that day. I'm certain I fell short because there are no words that can convey the magnitude of her spirit. I tried my best to answer that call, but I wasn't finished.

It was time to set The Tone.

I continued by explaining Melanie's go-to statement throughout her cancer battle: "Don't silver-line me!" It wasn't negative or pessimistic. It came from her realistic, practical approach. She spurned false hope, and that was part of her strength.

I explained that while I understood her approach, we did differ somewhat in this regard, as I do try to look on the bright side as much as I can. I said that while I don't mind someone silver-lining me, what I don't want, and won't tolerate, is pity.

I proclaimed that we didn't need anyone feeling sorry for us. We were lucky and blessed to have Melanie in our lives, and it was an honor and a privilege to spend these years with her. With her, I grew into a far better person than I ever would have been without her. Life had hit us with a devastating blow, which had staggered us, but it wouldn't defeat us. Ingrained with Melanie's spirit, we would band together and thrive, each in our own way. We would live extraordinary lives and continue striving to answer each call to make the world a better place, just as she always did. And just as she always did, with her spirit infused in us, we would have a lot of fun doing it. We would live in the spirit of Melanie.

I went back to the pew and sat back down with my kids. Even though the younger ones likely didn't understand most of what I had said, I somehow felt like The Tone of it wouldn't be lost on them. That was my main hope, and that was what I believed Melanie would want. Her kids were the most important thing to her, and she would want such a tone set for their lives. But it isn't just about setting a tone. If all you do is set a tone, then it's just words. We had to live The Tone.

Life was about to slap me in the face and immediately remind me what a challenge it is to live The Tone.

Within minutes, the service was drawing to a close. The funeral director walked across in front of the pews from the side of the sanctuary. I assumed he was going to act as usher and direct us to exit pew by pew, so I anticipated standing up. But instead of stepping up to us, he stepped up to the coffin. Why? What was he doing there? I hoped he was going to bow or make the sign of the cross or some similar gesture and move on, but he didn't. He reached up and grabbed the edge of the lid.

He couldn't be that stupid!

He wasn't really about to shut the mother of four small children into a box—four feet in front of the eyes of those children—*was he?*

I shot a horrified look across the aisle at Stephanie. I certainly can't say what she was thinking, but she sat rigidly with a look of strenuous composure on her face. Her gaze remained focused straight ahead. She seemed vigorously motionless, as if she were trying hard to look like she wasn't trying hard. Although different from Melanie in many ways, Stephanie also had an amazingly strong spirit of her own, and she maintained composure in even the most upsetting of situations—situations like this one. While I thought I detected the same sense of horror underlying her expression that I was feeling, it was her composure that revived my parental instincts. I instantly wiped the look of dismay off my face so that I didn't magnify the panic and horror for our children.

"What's he doing to Mommy?" one of our two youngest blurted out as the lid dropped down.

When the lid shut, the other of the two youngest cried out, "Mommy!"

One of our kids jumped immediately into my lap, and another snuggled against me in the pew. I pulled them close and hugged them both tightly. I think I said something to them, but I can't remember. If I did, it certainly wasn't anything helpful—certainly not anything that would alleviate the agony of the stupidity transpiring before us. What could I say about something like that, especially to children?

"It's okay, kids. He's just shutting your Mommy's dead carcass up in a box for the rest of eternity. He just thought you'd like this visual reminder to punctuate the dreadfulness of the loss of your mother."

Yeah, something like that.

Let it go. Move on.

Of course, moving on isn't easy. Living The Tone isn't easy. In the following weeks, I considered how to conform to the example Melanie set and how to stay focused on the positives. I realized the answer is all around me. Melanie wasn't the only extraordinary person I knew. There were plenty of extraordinary people all around me, already living The Tone, already answering the call.

If anyone had been watching us exit the church after her services, our congregation would have appeared completely ordinary. What I saw was our ordinarily extraordinary community.

Within several feet of me in that sanctuary, I saw brilliant engineers, chemists, doctors, nurses, teachers, lawyers, financial gurus, electricians, entrepreneurs, and numerous others blend into the crowd like ordinary folk. They are what inspires me the most. Melanie helped me learn to see the extraordinary aspects of ordinary life, especially the extraordinary people all around me. It's been right in front of me my entire life, but I had to learn to see it.

As much as I saw genius and accomplishment in that congregation of people flowing out of the sanctuary, I also saw so much of the same spirit of kindness, compassion, and fun that Melanie exemplified. As the community supported us in the months that followed, staggeringly generous gifts and overwhelming acts of kindness and compassion reinforced that conclusion, bolstering my appreciation of my family, friends, and community to extraordinary levels. Most of these people were not wealthy. This wasn't easy for them. They sacrificed to support us. They had busy lives and limited budgets. They were trying to manage their own finances, provide vacations and activities for their own kids, and yet they would spend their own money and time to provide support to us because they loved Melanie and her family. How could that not humble me?

I came to realize that it is a choice to see the good. I had to learn how to understand that it is a choice, and then I had to make a concerted effort to live by that choice. I came to understand that there is far more good than bad in this world. I used to focus on the bad.

Twenty good things would happen to me in a day, but when one bad thing happened, that's what I took home with me and vented about. The trick is to let it go, move on, and focus on the positive. While our societies still have plenty of problems to address, we have come so far. We need to continue to build upon that and support one another. I want to be a builder and a supporter. I want to contribute. Understanding all this, how can I not be stoked to live in this extraordinary ordinary that I've learned to see?

The community support, however, did get a little weird on at least one occasion. A woman I didn't know showed up unannounced at our door one day. She seemed a little flustered, saying she wanted to connect with us and help in some way because she loved Melanie so much. She offered to take the kids somewhere. I think she was sincere and well-intentioned, but I had no idea who she was. I didn't recall ever hearing her name before, and she didn't look familiar. She said she had worked with Melanie, explaining they had stayed in touch over the years and Melanie was the one person she could talk to about things, which didn't surprise me and actually provided some legitimacy. But I wasn't inclined to send my kids off with some random door knocker, no matter how nice she seemed. I wasn't about to watch them pile into some alien's car and drive off and hope there might be a decent possibility that she might actually bring them back.

Thanks, but we've already got plans today and they don't have time, and even if we don't really have plans today, I'm just gonna go ahead and tell you that we do.

Thanks for stopping by.

11

The Middle Pieces

O f all the positives in my life, the honor and privilege of raising our kids is my greatest blessing. I'm going to love my kids and cherish every moment I get to watch them grow and evolve into upstanding and phenomenal adults. Sometimes, I'm not going to worry about parenting them and just enjoy time with them and laugh with them. I can see Melanie's spirit infused in them, and with that, they are already off to a great start.

I have so many examples to show me why they are my greatest blessing. Melanie lost her mom at nine years old, and now Melanie's worst fear has come to pass and she isn't here to be with her kids. I appreciate that I am. I've seen many different situations of parents and children losing one another, whether from death or other circumstances. After the events that transpired leading to the adoption of a boy that may or may not have been mine, I lived every day of the last quarter of a century wondering if there was a child out there who was my son and wondering how he was doing. I still didn't know. In one of those crazy twists that life seems to enjoy throwing at you, I got the answer in a totally unexpected way.

A couple months after Melanie passed, I got a call late one evening shortly after putting the youngest kids to bed. It was one of my four brothers. After the usual greetings and chit-chat, his tone changed.

"Hey, uh…" He was hesitant. "This is awkward…"

I waited while a chill sauntered up my spine. I had absolutely no idea what he was about to say, but his tone was ominous.

"You know that ancestry DNA test I did a while back?"

I knew.

I finally knew.

That child *was* my son. That child was now a grown man, and he was my son. Those words were all it took to know.

I didn't need him to say it. If the child wasn't my son, if he had the DNA of some other man not related to us, nothing would have shown up in DNA testing, so my brother would know nothing. I instinctively realized that without even thinking it through. I wondered why he was telling me now. My brother had taken that test years earlier. Did he know all this time and was just telling me? If so, why did he choose to tell me now?

Despite realizing why he was calling, prudence told me to wait for him to say it. It could be something else. I didn't want to blurt out something unnecessarily. That would *really* be awkward.

"Well, their system alerts me to any new matches. A couple weeks ago, I got an email about a new match that said it was likely my nephew or grandson. I didn't get how that could be possible. There's a way in the system to send a message to a match, and he and I ended up writing back and forth. We figured out—"

"I know." I don't know if I actually cut him off. The conversation is rather blurred in my memory, but I remember it moved quickly. I told him the whole story—well, most of it. I told him how it transpired and why I never knew if the child was my son or not, but now DNA told us the answer.

My brother had debated telling me this news in the wake of Melanie's passing, but he had only recently found out. He was gracious about it all. He wasn't the slightest bit judgmental. We talked a bit longer, and it was a nice conversation.

I connected with the son I finally knew I had via text messages and started a dialog, but as of the time of this writing, I still haven't spoken with him or met him. He told me he wasn't ready for that. I totally respect that, but I don't claim to understand. I don't mean that in any bad or judgmental way. How could I understand? As much as we are connected in this, our situations are totally different.

I hope to talk to him someday. I hope to meet him. From his messages, he seems like a good, intelligent person. I'd like to know how his life has been. Does he have a good relationship with his adoptive parents, and did they treat him well? Did he have a good childhood? I wonder about these things all the time. I have been wondering every day for years.

I don't regret it. That would be like saying I wish he weren't in this world, and I certainly don't feel that way at all. It's complicated. I wish I could have known him and even raised him, but from the circumstances that developed, I still believe I made the best decision that I could have made at the time. I would not have been a good father back then. I couldn't even manage my own life, and at the time of his conception, I was disgusted with myself and hated the world around me, which isn't exactly conducive to a healthy family environment.

I'm a drastically different person now than I was then. I overcame a lot. I don't want to rationalize anything or make excuses for myself, but it appears that my irresponsible actions turned out to be a blessing in the lives of others, at least, I'm assuming and hoping that. I hope they shared a lot of love. I hope I get to find out some day. I'm glad I finally know. I'd love to get a call from him. I'd love to meet him. Whatever happens, I hope he's happy and living a good life.

One week after Melanie's funeral, we buried Daun. Stephanie buried her only sibling and then several days later buried her remaining parent. Her strength and spirit were amazing. In the months that followed, we grew closer, talking often and supporting one another as we trekked through all the muck of the grief. She showed me all the best of the human spirit. She didn't just persevere; she thrived and grew as a person. She lived The Tone in the spirit of Melanie, and she was there for others. It has been inspirational and uplifting to watch. Technically, I guess she isn't my sister-in-law any longer. Is that how that works? It doesn't matter. She is my sister. I don't even care about the "in-law" part. She's my sister. Allen, her husband, is my brother. Her daughters are my nieces. Our kids are cousins. We are family.

Two weeks after Melanie's funeral, I faced our 19th wedding anniversary. As it approached, and even when I woke up that day, I had no idea how to feel about it. Was it our anniversary? Technically, it *would have been* our wedding anniversary, but we weren't married any longer—is that right? What a bizarre concept. I couldn't wrap my head around it. Was I not married anymore? Death had "done us part"—I guess. Is that how it works? I had trouble comprehending the idea that I was single. Was I? How could I be? Was this day something to celebrate? How do you celebrate your wedding anniversary when you don't have a wife? Did I not have a wife? Was Melanie not my wife anymore? How could that be? I had questions. Lots of questions. I had no answers. Who was going to answer these questions?

The word *widower* came to mind. Of course, I couldn't be a widower. What a strange word. Is that really a word? What the hell does that word even mean? I thought of learning what that word meant as a kid. There was an old-man-dad in our community, and they called him a widower. Obviously, I couldn't be a widower. I wasn't a widower. I was a young married guy with his whole life ahead of him. Widower? That's something old-man-dads are. Wait…I was an old-man-dad. Shit. I was an old-man-dad. I was 50. I had four kids—actually five, I had now learned, but four I was raising. Damn, I was a widower. I was an old-man-dad widower.

Damn.

How the hell could that be? How did that happen? Who was I? What was I supposed to do now? I didn't know how to live as an old-man-dad widower. What does an old-man-dad widower do? Sounds like some sad and grumpy old guy who sits on a bench on his porch and yells at neighborhood kids for walking on his lawn. Some crass old man who cares more about his grass than his neighbors. I didn't even have a bench on my porch. I don't even fertilize my grass. I couldn't be an old-man-dad widower. I didn't know how. I didn't know what to do. I still feel like an immature kid most of the time.

My kids were in school on the day that was, or wasn't, our anniversary. I was working from home, just without the working part. I was sitting at the kitchen table. I decided I wasn't doing anything for this anniversary that maybe wasn't an anniversary. I had made a definite decision. I was certain that there was nothing to celebrate and nothing to commemorate. It was just another day. With that decision firmly made, I grabbed my car keys and got in the car to go to the cemetery.

How could I not spend time with Melanie on our anniversary?

I stopped at the McDonald's near our house for two reasons. I wanted a fountain, and I had to bring her one. I would get one for each of us—his-and-her fountains. I pulled up to the window. The woman at the window had been working there a few years. I didn't know her name, but I recognized her. She was always nice. I handed her my debit card.

"Where's that sweet wife of yours been? I haven't seen her in a while."

You've got to be kidding me! I wasn't ready for that. I didn't expect a question like this in the drive-thru. Tears filled my eyes, which I tried to fight off. There's no crying in drive-thrus!

"She passed away a couple weeks ago." My voice was shaking a little.

Tears welled up in the woman's eyes. "Oh, my dear Melanie. I'm so sorry." She started crying. She put her hand on her chest over her heart, and then she covered her mouth with her other hand.

You've got to be kidding me!

She knew her name! She started crying! *What was that?* How does someone elicit that strong of a reaction from the local drive-thru worker? But why did it surprise me? Melanie was a woman who befriended the bill collector. Perhaps I should expect things like this, but I didn't see it coming. It was the first and only time I ever cried buying a fountain, or any other fast-food menu item, for that matter. I'd been having a lot of firsts like that since Melanie passed, and there would be plenty more.

I drove out to the cemetery. It was nearly a 30-minute drive down one road. Manchester Road cut right through the middle of the West County of St. Louis, and I must have passed dozens of fast food restaurants along with other businesses. I wondered how many of them had workers who knew Melanie by name.

It was the first time I'd been to the cemetery since the funeral. I didn't know what to do. I never understood cemeteries. It always seemed like an odd and mostly pointless thing to visit a cemetery. The person wasn't there. This wasn't a place that was special to us. It's not like it's some place where we used to hang out together. It was just a bunch of grass and headstones. Why go there?

Melanie's grave didn't even have a headstone yet. They told me the ground needed six months to settle before putting it in place. She had been buried in the month of March. It's still cold in St. Louis in March, so no grass was growing. I came all the way out here to stare at a mound of dirt. Why did I bother?

The mount of dirt was uneven. There was a ridge at the far end where the dirt had sunk below the grass line. I set her fountain there where it could lean up against the little ridge. I stepped into the mound as I set the fountain there, and I left a footprint in the soft soil. Something seemed oddly appropriate about leaving my footprint on her grave. I didn't really think about it or try to interpret that feeling; I just felt it.

When I stepped back and saw my footprint and the fountain, I suddenly felt a connection to her. For the first time in my life, I had a sense of why we have cemeteries and why we visit them. It was the one place in the world dedicated to her and only her. It struck me that her body was only a few feet away beneath me. It felt like a strange and sad thought, but at the same time, it made me feel close to her. A surge of emotions consumed me.

It was like a sneeze, except that it came on even more quickly and more powerfully. I burst into a hysterical bout of crying. I felt ridiculous and stupid. I was crying over a mound of dirt.

"You were right…" I wailed. "I wish I had been nicer to you."

Over the years, when I was grumpy or annoyed, Melanie would matter-of-factly say to me that someday when she was gone, I'd wish I had been nicer to her. I'd roll my eyes and get annoyed with her for saying it. Back in the day, it seemed like a meaningless thing to say because you think everything will stay as it is forever. Your life is your life, and it seems like it is what it will always be. She must have said that to me dozens of times over the years, maybe hundreds. I think she said it less after she was diagnosed, probably because it became too real and morbid.

I was bawling over that mound of dirt. It had to look ridiculous if anyone was watching. But she was right—I wished I had been nicer to her. I felt so much regret, such depths of remorse. I thought about The Epic Hallway Failure, that day walking the H in the hospital when Melanie commented that I wouldn't sign up for this again. My failure haunted me. I had been annoyed with her and then almost nonchalant in my response. I felt what I said to her was good, but I couldn't shake the feeling that it would have been the perfect moment to show my love for her more passionately—show her the passion she would have wanted to see. I should have been Jerry Maguire in the living room, pouring out my heart. I should have been Lloyd Dobler, holding the boombox over my head. I blew the moment.

Maybe it wasn't just about that moment. While I felt like The Epic Hallway Failure was haunting me, maybe it was more about regret, realizing how much more I wish I'd said to her when I had the time, when I had the chance, before she was gone. I couldn't say anything to her anymore.

"*Where are you?*" I screamed at the mound. None of this made any sense. I couldn't comprehend it. I wanted her back, and I didn't understand how she could be gone. How could her lifeless body be buried under all this dirt, a few feet away, yet I couldn't see her or touch her or talk to her? I snapped into a rage. I wanted to hit something. I wanted to destroy something.

"How are you not here?" I screamed. I wanted answers. I didn't understand. I wanted someone to pay for this. I wanted the Grim Reaper to show up and explain to me why he took her. I wanted to pound his face into that mound of dirt and make him bring her back.

I collapsed onto my knees. The waves of anger subsided, but I was still crying uncontrollably. My eyes were burning, and I had a pounding headache once again.

I talked to Melanie for a while about a bunch of different things. I apologized for all kinds of things. The baggage of nearly 19 years of marriage. At one point, I started to get angry, but this time at her. As the surviving partner, I was mostly regretting my own actions, but then I realized that she had let me down at times as well. I quickly buried those thoughts. It wasn't because there wasn't truth in them— there was. I would need to process and deal with those feelings, but that could be done another time. This was our anniversary. That crap could wait. Instead, I talked to her about the kids, and I vowed to her that they would have great lives. I promised that they would know things about her, and that they would thrive.

I felt like I should have more to say, but I was running out of thoughts. I reached a point where the same thoughts rotated through my head, and it started to feel kind of stupid that I was repeating myself to a mound of dirt, so I decided it was time to go. I reluctantly walked back to the car. It was nearly as hard to leave that gravesite as it had been to leave her in the hospital when she died. The Crutcher caveat proved true again. Why was it so damn hard to leave a mound of dirt? Leaving would make it too real, as if she were only actually dead if I left, but she would miraculously reappear if I stayed.

I got into the car and sat there without starting it. My mind was spinning. I looked back at the grave. Was she really in that ground? What would happen if I left her? What would happen if I didn't? I shook the steering wheel frantically, as if I might rip it out.

"SUCK IT, TREBEK!" I screamed at no one, at everyone, at the steering wheel.

I don't feel I really understand the word "closure." To me, it implies closing, as an end of something that is done and over. There is no closure with Melanie. I suppose there is acceptance, but then just say "acceptance" and not "closure." My life with Melanie won't ever close or end. She is part of me. So much of me is formed out of her, even my vocabulary. Her life and her impact and her spirit are not closed, or done, or over. She lives on in us. She lives on in our kids, in our family, in our friends, and in our community. Shit, she even lives on in the drive-thru lady and the bill collector.

Her legacy and her impact will stay with us forever, shaping so much of the way we think and act. I am a drastically different person because of her influence in my life, and that will never come to a close. It will never end. It has already shaped our children's outlook and personalities, and it will remain with them forever and get passed on to their friends and their own children indefinitely. She was such an amazing influence on so many other people, having a positive impact everywhere she went. People like her are what keep making the world progressively better. Why can't there be more people like her? We should all try to be more like her. She answered the call every day of her life. She answered multiple calls every day.

Sitting in the car looking at her grave, I thought about another Melanie story. After Melanie's mom died, a new girl came to her school. They were both 10 years old. The girl was sitting on the side of the playground at recess crying. Melanie walked over and asked the girl what was wrong.

"Barb is being mean to me. She keeps making fun of me," the girl told Melanie.

"Oh, Barb's a bitch!" Melanie exclaimed. "Come play with me."

First of all, I'm proud of my girl for already mastering the use of her cuss words at such a young age. At 10, she was already utilizing the appropriate cuss words in the appropriate situation.

Impressive. My kind of girl.

Even more impressive, Melanie was already the extraordinary friend a complete stranger needed. Melanie was living with a crass and abusive father less than two years after her mother died of breast cancer. Melanie could have been lashing out. It wouldn't be out of the ordinary for a child who had dealt with all that to be the bully. Instead, Melanie was the friend that little girl needed. They played together and remained lifelong friends. That little girl would be one of her bridesmaids in our wedding.

I didn't get closure that day at the cemetery. I have never gotten closure, and I don't want it. I don't believe it's possible. I consider it a false concept, a misnomer. I think this day might have put me on a path to acceptance, but that would still be a long road ahead. The time I spent at her grave that day brought out a lot of thoughts, and that was a great thing, even if it was painful and distressing. I finally started the car and drove off, but the day wasn't over yet. I might have been on a path to acceptance, but I wasn't done celebrating our anniversary together in spirit.

I was starving. I had not eaten breakfast, and it was past noon. There were dozens of restaurants along Manchester Road on the drive back. I thought about which one I might go to for lunch, but then I realized where I had to go. I drove all the way back, past where I would turn to go to my house, and kept going. In a few more minutes, I pulled into the parking of O'B Clark's.

Well past one o'clock, the lunch crowd was mostly gone. Only a couple of people were sitting at tables, and a few old men sat at the bar. I wondered if they were the same old men who had been there over 20 years ago when Melanie and I had lunch there. I bet at least a couple of them were, and they were probably telling the same stories they were telling back then. Good for them. I hope when I'm an old man, I have friends to tell all my same old stories to over a beer.

It was now in a different building. The original O'B Clark's had been down the street in a strip mall that had been torn out to build a bigger shopping center. I guess things are always changing and evolving. This location had much the same look and feel, and the pizza was still the same. I ordered a pizza and sat there trying not to cry. The waitress came by, and I talked to her briefly. I don't have Melanie skills, so it wasn't much of a conversation, but it was nice and cordial. But then an older man a couple of tables away said something to me about the Blues, the St. Louis hockey team that was finishing the season strong and were on their way to winning the Stanley Cup for the first time in franchise history a couple months later. We talked the Blues for a few minutes, and then the conversation tapered off.

"Chief's fan, huh?" I asked him. He was wearing a Chiefs' hat. Pretty observant of me.

He jumped at the question and talked all about growing up in Kansas City. I channeled Melanie and let him talk about himself. It was fun to hear about his life. He had been a roofer, but his bad back forced him into retirement. He talked about the roofing industry for a few more minutes. I was in the process of getting a new roof since I'd found roofing shingles in my yard a couple weeks earlier. As smart as I am, I surmised that the roofing shingles weren't supposed to be in my yard, and I called a roofing company. He knew the one and said that was a good company. He talked a little about roofing until he somehow ended up back on the Chiefs. He said something about the Rams and asked me if I was a fan.

"I liked to see them do well, but I'm a Steelers' fan," I said. "Have been since I was a kid."

"Oh!" He perked up. "My little brother used to play for the Steelers!" He told me all about it. I'd never heard of his brother, but apparently, he was a backup running back in the 1960s. He only played a couple seasons and then went into insurance. He was clearly fond of his brother, whom he spoke about for a few minutes. It was a nice conversation, and he really seemed to enjoy telling me his stories. He left with a smile on his face shortly after my pizza arrived.

I ate the outer pieces and left the middle pieces for Melanie. She always liked the middle pieces. It felt like a silly little symbolic gesture, but it meant something to me. That's what it's all about—discovering what the middle pieces are for your partner or any of your loved ones and giving them unconditionally.

O'B Clark's has a back entrance and a front entrance, but from either side, you circled around into the parking lot. I'd come in the back, but I left out the front, leaving differently than I had arrived in more ways than one, just as I had over two decades ago.

I needed to do one thing before the kids got home from school. It was a little errand that had nothing to do with our anniversary or Melanie. I wove through a few residential streets until I came out on Litzsinger Road and turned right. I came to a stoplight at McKnight Road, and the light was red. When I passed through the intersection, I would be driving into Ladue, which is one of the richest zip codes in the country. It is home to people like members of the Busch family, of Anheuser-Busch beer-brewing fame and fortune. My little shortcut was a narrow two-lane street weaving through mansions in a heavily tree-lined neighborhood, so it almost felt like driving through the woods.

The moment the light turned green, a new song kicked in on the radio, and of all the damned things, it happened to be "Maybe I'm Amazed" by Paul McCartney. This was one of the songs I had, for years, daydreamed about learning to play on the piano and singing to Melanie someday. I always thought the words so perfectly portrayed how I felt about her and our relationship.

The moment I heard the first notes of that song, I let out an inhuman wail. On this day of our anniversary, after spending time at the cemetery and O'B Clark's, this song was both the perfect ending for this celebration and the worst possible torment for my soul. As I drove down the windy tree-lined street, I bellowed out the words hideously. I am not a good singer, and I was bawling and howling the words out at the top of my lungs.

It must have been absolutely *dreadful*. My guttural screeching of those words must have been utterly gruesome and revolting. I would not have permitted the torture of listening to my yowling upon my worst enemy. If I had been on a busier street, I don't think I could have had this moment. I would have been too embarrassed to be seen like that. It would have terrified small children. Hell, it probably would have terrified adults as well.

As I sang the words, I became even more aware of how perfectly composed the lyrics were for our relationship, with only one small inaccuracy—the word "maybe." There was no maybe about it. I was afraid. I didn't understand. I felt crushed.

This is a perfect example of why I am not a rah-rah cheerleader. While I'm determined to live The Tone, and I'm committed to living in the spirit of Melanie, I'm not pretending it's easy. We all have our moments. Moments of doubt. Moments of anxiety. Moments of stress. Moments of pain. These moments can be excruciating and can seem insurmountable, but they aren't. We get through them, often with a little help from our friends, and then we regroup and take on the next challenge. What specifically helps me through the tough times is reflecting on how awesome the world really is. The amazing accomplishments that have improved our world, and the amazing people that enrich it. I take inspiration from the ordinarily extraordinary all around me, and I look forward to the myriad blessings that it will continue to offer.

On my drive, I was crying so profusely that I could barely see. I probably should have been arrested for operating a motor vehicle in that condition. It was eerily perfect to experience that song at that exact moment, but it was agonizing.

I came to Old Warson Road and turned right. I was now on the exact reverse path that I'd driven home from the grocery store when Melanie had the speech stroke that kicked this whole series of events into motion. I was on that path because I was going to that grocery store.

It might look like a literary device to end the book this way, as if I'm making this up to bring the story full circle, but that is not the case. I actually went to the grocery store that day. At the time, I had no idea that this would be the ending of a book because I didn't know I'd be writing this book. There was one reason why I was going there.

Because life goes on.

We needed groceries, and life didn't care what happened to me. Life didn't care that I was hurting. Life didn't care that I was hideously wailing in my car in soul-wrenching torment. The kids still needed to be fed. Laundry still had to be folded. Dishes still had to be washed. Floors still had to be swept, and so on and so forth.

We needed milk and bread and a few other things. On this trip, I wouldn't be going to the pharmacy for the first time in what seemed like forever. I wondered if the pharmacists would start noticing that I wasn't coming around. I wondered if they'd miss me.

I sat in my car for a few minutes in the parking lot, trying to stop crying. My head felt like it was splitting open and my eyes were burning—yet again. I took some deep breaths and then finally got out of my car and walked in. I walked into the grocery store to pick up some bread and milk. Somewhere between the apples and bananas, not too far from the rhubarb, my phone rang. I pulled it out of my pocket. I smiled when I saw who it was on the caller ID. It was someone I'd been wanting to talk to.

I answered the call.

You should too.

About the Author

Patrick P. Long is a father and widower born and raised in St. Louis, MO. While pursuing his lifelong ambition of being a writer, Patrick has earned his living as a systems' engineer and database architect, which means he is a nerdy computer programmer.

Patrick has passions for aviation, sports, reading, writing, theater, music, movies, and popcorn. He eats way too much pizza and buffalo wings. He likes to binge-watch really good television shows.

Patrick has trained as a pilot and flown an airplane solo. He completed a grueling 24-hour adventure race with four of his most insane friends. In training, Patrick flipped over the handlebars of his mountain bike and smashed face-first into a tree, somehow managing not to break his nose or knock out any teeth. What is even more embarrassing and he doesn't want to admit is that he did it again a week later.

Patrick's wife, Melanie, passed from breast cancer in 2019. Patrick is an avid supporter of the American Cancer Society and also Camp Kesem, a phenomenal camp and a child's friend through and beyond a parent's cancer.

Made in the USA
Monee, IL
18 June 2021